Deadly Women
Volume Four

18 Shocking
True Murder Cases

Robert Keller

**Please Leave Your Review of This Book At
http://bit.ly/kellerbooks**

ISBN-13: 978-1722342548

ISBN-10: 1722342544

© 2018 by Robert Keller

robertkellerauthor.com

All rights reserved.

No part of this publication may be copied or reproduced in any format, electronic or otherwise, without the prior, written consent of the copyright holder and publisher. This book is for informational and entertainment purposes only and the author and publisher will not be held responsible for the misuse of information contain herein, whether deliberate or incidental.

Much research, from a variety of sources, has gone into the compilation of this material. To the best knowledge of the author and publisher, the material contained herein is factually correct. Neither the publisher, nor author will be held responsible for any inaccuracies.

Table of Contents

Kelly Cochran 5
Martha Marek 13
Larissa Schuster 21
Audrey Marie Hilley 27
Melissa Ann Friedrich 37
Dorothea Waddingham 43
Inessa Tarverdiyeva 49
Debora Green 55
Anna Zwanziger 65
Karla Faye Tucker 71
Karen Lee Huster 79
Mary Ann Cotton 85
Blanche Taylor Moore 93
Martha Rendell 99
Michelle Knotek 105
Terri Rachals 113
Katherine Knight 125

Kelly Cochran

Christopher Regan was missing, and the police in the small Michigan town of Iron River were baffled as to his whereabouts. Regan's car had been found abandoned at a Park-n-Ride in October 2014. No crime there. An adult is entitled to drop out of sight if that is what he or she chooses to do. Many follow that path, for their own reasons. But in Regan's case, it just did not make sense. The 53-year-old military contractor had recently landed a new job in North Carolina and had been planning his move there. According to friends, he'd been excited at the prospect of starting anew. Moreover, the divorced father of two maintained a close relationship with his children and would never have gone anywhere without letting them know.

So what had happened to Regan? Friends and acquaintances of the missing man offered at least one interesting snippet of information. They said that Chris had been having an affair with a married woman, 35-year-old Kelly Marie Cochran. A handwritten note that had been found inside Regan's car seemed to confirm this. And once detectives checked Regan's cell phone records and found numerous calls between him and Cochran, they knew where they had to begin their investigation.

Kelly Cochran wasn't difficult to find. In fact, she and the missing man had been co-workers. Questioned about their relationship, she readily admitted that they had been sleeping together. According to Kelly, her husband, Jason, knew all about it and had given his approval, as long as it was purely about sex, with no emotional attachments. As for Chris Regan's whereabouts, Kelly said that she had no idea where he might be. They'd recently ended the affair after Chris told her that he was moving out of state.

The next port-of-call for detectives was the Cochran residence to interview the unemployed Jason Cochran. As the potentially wronged husband, Jason certainly had motive. But he backed up everything his wife had said. According to him, he'd been injured in an accident that had rendered him impotent. He'd then given his wife permission to take a lover, provided the relationship remained purely physical. He'd done this, he said, because he was afraid that Kelly might leave him for someone else if her physical needs were not met. He also claimed that he bore no ill will towards his wife's lover and that Chris had even been a dinner guest in their home. Furthermore, Jason offered an alibi for the day of Chris's disappearance. He said that he had been in the hospital receiving treatment for "anxiety."

Kelly had been a convincing witness, her husband less so. The police did not believe his story and therefore obtained a search warrant for the couple's home. They need not have bothered. Kelly willingly invited them in and told them that they were welcome to look wherever they liked. She seemed almost smug when the search turned up nothing. Later, the police would learn that she had taken college-level classes in forensics and thus might have known what was required to clean up a crime scene.

But while the search might have come up empty, the Cochrans' next act certainly aroused suspicion. Shortly after they were interrogated by the police, the couple suddenly packed their bags and moved to Indiana. They departed in the middle of the night, leaving behind furniture, personal belongings, even the food in their refrigerator. When the police later questioned neighbors about the couple's sudden departure, they garnered still more suspicious details. On the night of October 27, the night Chris Regan had vanished, there had been strange noises coming from the Cochran residence. A neighbor described it as "the sound of sawing" and said that it had continued until well after midnight. When the neighbor asked Jason about it the next morning, he'd said that he had been unable to sleep and had been working on building a staircase. The only problem with that explanation was that none of the Cochrans' neighbors could recall seeing any lumber being delivered to the house.

And then there was another story, one that would ensure the infamy of this case for years to come. A neighbor, David Saylor, reported a number of unprecedented dinner invitations in late October. Previously, the Cochrans had barely exchanged greetings with him and his wife. Now they were invited three times in the space of a week, twice for a sit-down meal and once for a barbeque.

"There was so much meat," Saylor told police, "and barely any side dishes." He also said that the meat tasted like nothing he'd eaten before. "Not quite pork and not quite chicken" was how he described it. Only later, when Regan's disappearance came to light, did he consider the horrific possibility. "I'm thinking, oh, my God, did they cut this guy up?" Later, he'd tell a relative, "Dude, we ate dude!"

While David Saylor's revelations hinted at some horrific possibilities, they did not amount to evidence of murder. In truth, the police had nothing to link the Cochrans to Chris Regan's disappearance. Nothing, at least, that would stand up in a court of law. The matter remained, officially, a missing persons case. It would likely have stayed so but for another murder, committed 16 months later in Hobart, Indiana.

On the night of February 20, 2016, a 911 dispatcher in Lake County, Indiana, received a call from a woman who said that her husband had overdosed on heroin and wasn't breathing. Police and paramedics rushed to the scene and found 37-year-old Jason Cochran dead of an apparent overdose. His wife explained that she'd come home to find him lying dead on the floor.

Unfortunately for Kelly Cochran, the autopsy results did not back up her story. Her husband did have a large amount of heroin in his system, enough, possibly, to have caused an overdose. Except, he hadn't died of an overdose. He'd been asphyxiated. That put Kelly solidly in the frame, making her the one and only suspect.

Officers were immediately dispatched to bring Kelly Cochran in for questioning. But they arrived to find the Cochran residence empty and Kelly long gone. A manhunt was then launched. Since it was believed that the fugitive had fled across state lines, the FBI was brought into the investigation at this time. Their expertise in these matters would soon pay dividends as Cochran was tracked to Kentucky and arrested within a week.

Kelly Cochran was brought back to Indiana where, despite the evidence against her, she refused to admit to killing her husband. She continued to insist that Jason had died of an overdose. Then, after being shown the autopsy report, she changed her tune. She now conceded that he might have asphyxiated but continued to deny her involvement. "If he did suffocate, it must have happened accidentally, while he was passed out," she said. She challenged the police to prove otherwise. Doing so, they knew, would be a difficult challenge.

But then, one of the investigators suggested a ruse to finally break down Cochran's resistance. The FBI had by now learned that Kelly was a suspect in the disappearance of Chris Regan in Michigan. They had obtained the Regan case file and, armed with this information, they told Cochran that they had searched her home and found a letter left behind by Jason. In it, he'd admitted that he and Kelly had murdered Chris Regan and dismembered the body.

The letter was a fiction, of course, but the level of detail officers were able to provide convinced Kelly that it was real. She now admitted that she had killed Jason. According to her, she'd deliberately given him an overdose of heroin, hoping that it would kill him. But Jason was taking too long to die and so she'd suffocated him by squeezing his nose shut and holding her hand over his mouth. She had held this position until he'd stopped breathing. Only then had she called 911. She'd done it, she said, because Jason had killed Chris, who she described as "the only good thing in my life."

Explaining the motive for the Regan murder, Kelly said that she and Jason had a deal in place whereby they could sleep with whoever they liked, provided they did not form an emotional attachment. They had also agreed that should either of them fall in love with one of their affairs, they would act together to murder that person. She claimed that she'd always thought that Jason was joking about that part of the arrangement. However, after she had admitted to Jason that she had feelings for Chris, he had invoked the clause and insisted that she participate in Chris's murder.

Kelly had reluctantly agreed. On October 27, 2014, she lured Chris to her home in Iron River with the promise of sex. There, Jason shot him to death. They later dismembered the body and disposed of the remains in the woods of Michigan's Upper Peninsula. Then they cleaned up the crime scene before driving Chris's car to the Park-n-Ride where it would later be found.

Kelly would later lead the police to the spot where they'd dumped Chris's body. Various bones, including the skull, were discovered there, but it was far from a complete corpse. Cochran was coy as to what had happened to the rest of the remains. She refused to confirm or deny whether she'd fed her former lover's flesh to unsuspecting neighbors.

Kelly Cochran was ultimately sentenced to life in prison for the murder of Chris Regan. She subsequently made a deal with prosecutors in Indiana, pleading guilty to her husband's murder and accepting a 65-year prison term. But this is far from the end of the story. Details have since emerged that Cochran might have been involved in other murders and may be a serial killer. Kelly herself has done nothing to dampen this speculation. In fact, she has at various times confessed to killing 21 people.

These claims are, in all likelihood, an exaggeration. But investigators do believe that Kelly Cochran is responsible for more than the two murders of which she has been convicted. In the words of one officer, "There are probably others out there."

Martha Marek

As insurance frauds go, this one was pretty audacious. Emil Marek had decided to chop off his leg in order to claim against an accident policy. The plan was to make it look like the axe had slipped while he was cutting wood, but after striking the initial blow, Marek collapsed in agony. The cut had inflicted a deep gash on his shin, but it was not enough for his purposes. He, therefore, through gritted teeth, instructed his young wife Martha to finish the job. She delivered two more strikes on the damaged appendage, then rushed to call the doctor.

Emil Marek was transported to the hospital at Moedling, Austria, where it was determined that the leg hung on by no more than a sinew. It would have to be amputated. The following day, June 13, 1925, Mrs. Marek contacted the Anglo-Danubian Lloyd Company in Vienna and lodged a claim against the $400,000 policy.

The insurers were not pleased. Marek had only bought the policy a week earlier and had paid only one premium. They launched an inquiry and soon learned from the surgeon who had performed Emil's amputation that the injury could not have occurred the way the Mareks had described it. There were, in fact, three distinct cuts to the shin. What man would have the fortitude to hack three times into his own shin with an axe? The insurance claim was thus rejected. Not only that, but the Mareks found themselves charged with fraud.

The trial was set for December 1926. But the Mareks were not about to give up their windfall without a fight. Roping in the help of a hospital orderly, Karl Mraz, they concocted a new plan. Mraz was bribed to testify that he'd seen a doctor at the hospital inflict two additional wounds to the severed shinbone, the implication being that the doctor was on the payroll of the insurance company. This deception might well have worked, but then Mraz got greedy and demanded more money. When the Mareks refused, he went to the police and reported their attempt to defraud their insurer. The Mareks now found themselves arrested for the additional charge of bribery.

After several delays, the trial eventually got underway on March 28, 1927. Public opinion was staunchly behind the Mareks, who were deemed to be the victims of a big corporation's strong-arm tactics. Perhaps mindful of this, the insurance company agreed to an out-of-court settlement of $50,000. But most of that was gobbled up by the Mareks' legal fees, and they still had a bribery charge to face. Found guilty on that charge, they were each sentenced to four months in prison, although the time they'd spent in custody awaiting trial meant that they were released immediately.

It was a victory of sorts, but the harsh reality was that the Mareks had gained just $6,000 from a scheme that had left Emil an invalid. And that windfall was quickly whittled away on a series of hare-brained business schemes. By 1930, the couple was destitute again, and they now had the additional burden of a child to feed.

In 1932, Martha gave birth to a second child, and the family was forced to move from their Moedling villa to a far less salubrious neighborhood. Adding to their woes, Emil became ill in early July and was dead by the end of the month, apparently of tuberculosis. Martha Marek cashed in an insurance policy on his life. She received another payoff when her baby daughter, Ingeborg, died on September 2. Then her son, Alfons, also became ill, although he later recovered. Martha had identified a more lucrative target.

Suzanne Lowenstein was Martha Marek's great-aunt, the 67-year-old widow of an army officer. In the spring of 1934, Martha reached out to Mrs. Lowenstein, offering to care for her in her old age. The old lady was flattered by the interest and so impressed by Martha's devoted care that she quickly made her the sole beneficiary of her estate. That was a mistake. Within a month, Suzanne Lowenstein was dead, and Martha became the proud owner of a well-appointed home on the Kuppelwiesergasse.

But Martha Marek had never had a head for money, and it wasn't long before this latest windfall had been sufficiently eroded so that she had to take in boarders. One of those was an insurance agent named Jens Neumann who became her lover; another was a 53-year-old seamstress named Felicitas Kittenberger.

In short order, Martha had prevailed upon Neumann to write a life insurance policy on Mrs. Kittenberger with Martha as the sole beneficiary. Then a familiar pattern of events unfolded. Mrs. Kittenberger became ill, her eyesight failed, she lost the use of her limbs, her hair began falling out. By June 2, she was dead. Four days later, Marek collected a cash payment of $785.

Kittenberger's relatives, however, were not about to let the matter lie. Her son Herbert, in fact, called on the Marek home and accused Martha of poisoning his mother. Cool as ever, Martha called the police and laid a charge of trespass. Herbert Kittenberger was led angrily away, still spouting accusations. He was later released and warned to stay away from Marek.

One might think that this close call would have shaken Martha Marek up. Instead, the brazen murderess was emboldened by her narrow escape and began plotting her next caper. This involved not a murder, but an oft-worked insurance scam. Martha had inherited a number of valuable paintings and tapestries from her aunt's estate. Many of these pieces she'd already sold off, but she now decided to cash in again. The valuables had been previously insured for $2,200. In October 1936, she phoned the police and reported a theft.

The detective sent to investigate the robbery was Rudolph Peternell, a junior officer in the Vienna police force. Peternell was immediately suspicious of Marek's demeanor. She walked awkwardly, dragging her right leg and with her right arm dangling lifelessly by her side. Asked about her condition, Marek said that she had recently suffered a stroke. This surprised Peternell. Martha Marek sometimes supplemented her income by performing as a cabaret singer, and he'd just that morning read a newspaper article on a performance she'd given. She'd looked well enough in the accompanying picture.

His suspicions thus aroused, Inspector Peternell began looking into Marek's background. He learned that she had been born in Sopron, Hungary, 38 years earlier and had been adopted at an early age. Her adoptive father, Rudolph Lowenstein, had later abandoned the family, and Martha had been sent to a charitable institution in Vienna. At age 12, she'd been returned to her adoptive mother and had begun working as an errand girl in a dress shop.

Slim and dark-haired, Martha was a very pretty girl, and in 1911, when she was 13, she caught the eye of a wealthy department store owner named Moritz Fritsch. With the approval of Martha's mother, she became his ward, moving into his luxurious villa in fashionable Moedling. Fritsch pampered Martha and paid for a top class education that included finishing schools in England and France. In exchange, the teenaged Martha became her 62-year-old patron's lover. When Fritsch died in August 1923, he left the bulk of his estate to her.

Three months after Fritsch's death, the newly wealthy Martha met and married Emil Marek, then an engineering student at the Vienna Technical Institute. And here things really got interesting for Inspector Peternell. He learned how Martha and her new husband had squandered Moritz Fritsch's fortune on a succession of grandiose, but ultimately unsuccessful, schemes; he learned about Emil Marek's crudely amputated leg and the subsequent court case; he learned of the four suspicious deaths linked to Martha Marek.

In the meantime, another line of inquiry had also borne fruit. Peternell was able to track down the dealers who had bought items from Marek, items that she was now claiming as stolen. Marek soon found herself under arrest and charged with fraud.

But that was the least of Martha's problems. The bodies of Emil Marek, Ingeborg Marek, Suzanne Lowenstein and Felicitas Kittenberger had been exhumed and found to contain large quantities of thallium, a substance commonly used as rat poison at the time. Marek had been found to be a frequent purchaser of the poison, based on the registers kept by local pharmacists.

Martha Marek when on trial for four counts of murder on May 2, 1938, drawing large crowds to the Vienna courthouse. Those who were lucky enough to get a seat in the courtroom were treated to a number of feisty exchanges between Martha (dubbed the "Devil in Petticoats," by the media) and the State's Attorney. Marek was warned that she faced the death penalty if found guilty and urged to confess in exchange for a lighter sentence. She stoutly refused.

In the end, that was to prove a foolhardy decision. The case against her was overwhelming, with over 100 witnesses called for the prosecution. It was no surprise when she was eventually found guilty and sentenced to death.

The sentence handed down to Martha Marek was somewhat of a moral quandary to Austria's lawmakers. No woman had been executed in the country for over 60 years, and many expected Marek's sentence to be commuted. Austria, however, had recently been incorporated into Germany by Hitler's Anschluss, and the death penalty had been returned to the statute books.

And so it was that, on December 6, 1938, Martha Marek was led onto the scaffold before the newly erected guillotine. In the days leading up to her execution, Martha had claimed paralysis. She'd had to be pushed around in a wheelchair. Now, though, there was no sign of her affliction. She wrestled with the guards and managed to land a kick on executioner Johann Reichhart before she was subdued and forced to kneel. Then the blade fell and neatly removed her head.

Larissa Schuster

Larissa Foreman was born in 1960 and raised on a farm in Clarence, Missouri. She was a bright and driven girl who excelled at school and was later accepted at the University of Missouri, where she majored in biochemistry. During an internship at a nursing home, she met and fell in love with Timothy Schuster, a nursing student. The couple was married in 1982. Three years later, Larissa gave birth to a daughter, Kristin. In 1990, a son, Tyler, completed the happy family. By then they were living in Fresno, California, having moved there when Larissa was offered a high-paying job with an agricultural research company. Subsequently, she started her own successful business, Central California Research Laboratories.

On the face of it, the Schusters were living the dream. Larissa was earning good money, allowing them to buy a luxury home in Clovis, California. Tim, meanwhile, was working as an administrator at the nearby St. Agnes Medical Center, earning about half of Larissa's income. Not that it bothered him. A mild-mannered individual, Tim seemed content to let Larissa "wear the pants" in the relationship. He happily picked up the househusband duties of ferrying the kids to doctor's appointments, music lessons, and soccer games.

But by 2002, cracks had begun to appear. Kristin had grown into a willful teenager, and she and her mother clashed constantly. Over time, the situation deteriorated to such an extent that Larissa packed her daughter off to live with her grandparents in Missouri. There were strains on the marriage, too. Tim was aggravated by the long hours his wife put into her business. For her part, Larissa complained openly to acquaintances about Tim's impotence. To close friends, she admitted that she'd had an affair as far back as 1993.

Matters eventually came to a head in February 2002 when Larissa filed for divorce. Tim had no problem with that, but he insisted that he would remain in the family home until a settlement could be reached regarding the division of their shared assets. The couple began sleeping in separate bedrooms until the animosity between them eventually drove Tim out. He left in the summer of 2002 while Larissa was in Missouri visiting family. When she returned, she was infuriated to find that he'd taken items of furniture that she felt were rightfully hers.

In August 2002, Larissa persuaded a young man who worked at her lab, James Fagone, to help her break into Tim's apartment to retrieve the "stolen" items. Tim must have known who was responsible, but he never reported the break-in to the police. Instead, he bought himself a handgun. Larissa, meanwhile, continued to fume about her ex-husband. She harassed him with abusive phone calls and spoke openly about wanting him dead. No one suspected that she might actually follow through on her rants.

But Larissa had by now gone way beyond the point of mere threats. In July 2003, she began talking to James Fagone (the young man who had helped her burglarize Tim's apartment the previous year) about paying Tim a return visit. Only this time, she said, they would have to do the job while Tim was in the apartment as he had since installed a home security system. Gullible and trusting, Fagone agreed to help her.

With her accomplice on board, Larissa stepped up her plan. She instructed Fagone to buy a stun gun and some zip-ties while she put in a large order for hydrochloric acid to be delivered to her lab. She also placed an order for chloroform.

On the night of Thursday, July 9, 2003, Larissa called Fagone and told him to be ready. She was on her way to pick him up. Fagone waited on his boss's arrival, and Larissa then drove them to Tim's condo in Clovis, getting there at around 2 a.m. Friday morning. The pair entered the building and waited just outside the door while Larissa called Tim from her cell phone. She told him that their son, Tyler, was sick and that she needed Tim to come to his front door immediately. When Tim appeared moments later, Fagone zapped him with the stun gun. Larissa then pushed Tim back into the apartment, followed him in, and placed a chloroform-soaked rag over his mouth and nose. Tim was out in an instant. Larissa then instructed Fagone to bind Tim's hands and feet with the zip-ties and to help her carry him down to the car.

With her husband trussed up in the trunk, Larissa Schuster and her accomplice drove back to her home. There, they loaded Tim Shuster's body into a blue 55-gallon plastic drum. It is uncertain whether Tim was alive or dead when his wife started pouring out the containers of hydrochloric acid over his body.

The murder had been thought out in great detail. But Larissa had given much less thought to handling its aftermath. Tim was missed almost immediately as he had recently been laid off from his job and was due to have an exit interview on that Friday morning. His friend, Mary Solis, had arranged to meet him for breakfast afterwards. When he didn't show, Mary was immediately concerned. Tim was the most punctual and reliable man she knew.

A round of calls to friends and acquaintances got Mary no closer to tracking down Tim, so she waited the requisite 24 hours and then reported him missing to the police. A search of Tim's apartment instantly raised a red flag. His watch, wallet, and cell phone were sitting on the bedside table. It was unlikely that he'd have left without them. The search turned up something else, too. Several abusive and threatening messages were found on his answering machine, all of them from his wife, Larissa. Even more interesting was the call Larissa had made to Tim in the early hours of July 10. That call, made on the night that Tim when missing, immediately pushed her to the top of the suspect list.

Larissa was brought in for questioning but denied any involvement in Tim's disappearance. According to her, she hadn't seen Tim for several weeks and had had no contact with him at all. The detectives then confronted her with the call she'd made to Tim on July 10, but Larissa was quick on her feet. She said that she probably pressed the speed dial on her cellphone by accident, possibly by rolling over onto the phone while she was asleep. That might have been difficult to disprove except for one small detail. Tim's number had not been assigned a speed dial code on her phone.

The police picked up one other detail while checking Larissa's cellphone, the frequently-dialed number of James Fagone. While Larissa jetted off with her son for a planned family vacation at Disneyworld, detectives picked up Fagone and brought him in for questioning. They noticed immediately that he appeared fidgety and nervous under interrogation, and so they turned up the heat. It wasn't long before the young man cracked and blurted out the whole story. Larissa was the mastermind, he insisted. He had only gone along with the plan because she was his boss and because he was afraid of her.

With evidence now linking Larissa Schuster to the disappearance of her husband, the police had no problem obtaining search warrants for her home, office, and a storage locker she rented in Fresno. It was here that investigators made a truly horrific discovery. A blue plastic barrel stood to the rear of the unit. The container had been securely sealed, but that could not contain the eye-watering stench that emanated from it. It was with great trepidation that detectives levered off the lid from the container. Inside was the partially destroyed body of Tim Schuster, the head, arms and torso already dissolved, the legs still marinating in a vile-smelling gruel.

And so, less than a week after committing what she thought was the perfect crime, Larissa Shuster and her accomplice were taken into custody and charged with murder. James Fagone would be tried first. He got life in prison without parole, despite the jury's recommendation for leniency.

At her trial, Larissa took the stand to insist that she had played no part in the murder and that Fagone had acted alone. The jury did not believe her. She, too, was sentenced to life without parole. The "Acid Lady" is currently incarcerated at Valley State Prison for Women in Chowchilla, California.

Audrey Marie Hilley

The tiny Alabama town of Blue Mountain has a sinister claim to fame. It is the birthplace of two of America's most notorious Black Widows. One of these deadly women is Nannie Doss, the infamous "Giggling Granny" who went on to murder eleven members of her family across Alabama, North Carolina, Kansas, and Oklahoma. The other is Audrey Marie Hilley whose story is, if anything, more remarkable.

Born during the Great Depression, on June 4, 1933, Marie was the much-loved daughter of Huey and Lucille Frazier, hard-working local folk who were often forced to leave Marie in the care of relatives while they put in long hours at their respective jobs. As if to compensate for this, they spoilt the child rotten (or at least to the extent that they were able on their meager wages). Marie was always neatly and prettily turned out in clothes that were better than those of her peers. She also got her way in most things and was prone to throwing temper tantrums if anything was denied to her.

Yet, despite her sometimes bratty behavior, Marie grew to be a pretty, outgoing, and intelligent girl. In 1945, her parents moved to nearby Anniston where Marie began 7th grade at Quintard Junior High School. There, she came into contact with kids from the city's wealthiest families, the sons and daughters of mill owners and of local businesses. Not that Marie was in any way intimidated. Despite her own humble roots, she fit right in. At the end of that year, she was voted the prettiest girl at the school. Later, at Anniston High, she was a popular student who attracted much attention from the male contingent.

But Marie had eyes for only one. His name was Frank Hilley, a boy from a background similar to her own. Huey and Lucille, who'd hoped that their daughter might land a beau from one of Anniston's moneyed families, were disappointed in her choice. They tried to discourage her from becoming too serious with Frank, but Marie, as always, stood her ground. When Frank joined the Navy after graduation, she followed him out to California. Later, she moved with him to Boston and married him there in May 1951. By the time they returned to Alabama the following year, Marie was 19 years old and pregnant with her first child. Her son, Michael, was born on November 11, 1952.

To anyone looking from the outside in, the Hilleys appeared to be a happy family. Frank had a job in the shipping department at Standard Foundry while Marie worked as a secretary, and Michael spent his days in the care of his doting grandmother. Frank became a member of the Elks and the local chapter of Veterans of Foreign Wars; Marie was active in the church. Behind the scenes, though, trouble was brewing. Marie liked to splurge on material possessions, and her spending usually outstripped the family income. Even Frank's increased wage, after his promotion to supervisor, couldn't keep pace with his wife's extravagances.

In 1960, Marie gave birth to a second child, a daughter who she and Frank named Carol. Carol would grow up to be the apple of her father's eye, a situation which appeared to irk Marie. She was also annoyed that Carol turned out to be a bit of a tomboy, whereas she wanted her daughter to be demure and ladylike. Marie's relationship with Frank was also under strain. She liked to taunt him with love letters that she claimed to have received from male admirers. And her reckless spending went on unabated. Then, in April of 1974, Frank returned early from work and caught Marie in bed with her boss, Walter Clinton. Still deeply in love with his wife, Frank was devastated by the betrayal. Soon, his broken heart would be the least of his troubles.

During the Fall of 1974, Frank Hilley found that he was constantly tired and prone to frequent bouts of vomiting. He put this down to the pressure he was under at work, to money troubles, and perhaps to the chemicals he'd been exposed to at the foundry. Initially, he sought to tackle his symptoms with Alka-Seltzer, but by May, he was in such poor health that he finally went to see his family physician. However, nothing that the doctor prescribed for him seemed to help. On May 22, Frank was rushed to the hospital where tests showed that his liver had failed. Infectious hepatitis was diagnosed, but the prescribed medication had no effect. Frank's condition steadily worsened. He was jaundiced, hallucinating, and obviously in great pain. At one point, he had to be restrained from jumping out of a window. At around 5:00 a.m. on the morning of May 25, Frank's son Mike arrived to check on him and found him dead, with Marie fast asleep in a chair beside his bed. Cause of death was given as hepatitis.

Frank Hilley was buried on May 27, 1975. Thereafter, his widow cashed in the $31,000 that was due to her on his insurance policy and went on a spending spree. There was a new car, clothes, and jewelry for herself; a diamond ring for her mother; clothes and appliances for Michael; a car and a stereo for Carol. The money, worth around $165,000 in today's currency, didn't last long.

After Frank's death, Marie's mother, Lucille, came to live with Marie and Carol. Her grown son, Michael, also moved in for a time, bringing his new wife, Teri, with him. But Teri soon started suffering from nausea, stomach cramps and vomiting, symptoms very similar to those experienced by Frank Hilley. She was rushed to the hospital on at least four occasions, suffering a miscarriage on the last visit. That was too much for Frank to take, and he and Teri moved out soon after. Then Lucille was struck down by the same mystery illness. She died in January 1977, although no suspicion was attached to the death since she had been diagnosed with cancer two years earlier.

In August 1978, Marie Hilley was again shopping for life insurance, taking out a $25,000 policy on her daughter, Carol, who was by then 19 years old and a freshman in college. Within a month, Carol began complaining of nausea, an affliction so bad that she was admitted to the emergency room on several occasions. Doctors were perplexed by her condition, particularly as nothing they prescribed seemed to alleviate the symptoms. Things got so bad that in mid-1979, Marie gave her daughter an injection that she said would alleviate the nausea. She claimed that she had been given the medication by a friend of hers who was a registered nurse. But the injection did not help. In fact, it made things worse. Carol started complaining about numbness in her hands and feet and was taken to hospital for further tests.

But still, the attending physicians could not find the source of Carol's ailment. They even began to suspect that her symptoms might be psychosomatic and recommended a transfer to Carraway Methodist Hospital in Birmingham, Alabama, where she could undergo psychiatric evaluation. While Carol was there, Marie twice gave her shots of the mystery drug that she claimed to have received from her nursing friend. She warned Carol not to say anything as that would get her friend into trouble.

About a month after Carol was admitted to Carraway Methodist, doctors called Marie in for a conference and told her that they now suspected that Carol was suffering from heavy metal poisoning. Marie was vehement in her rejection of that theory and, that same afternoon, had Carol transferred to the University of Alabama Hospital in Birmingham. But Carol's medical file accompanied her on that journey, and doctors at the University hospital immediately started testing for heavy metals. The symptoms certainly matched the diagnosis. Carol's hands and feet were numb, she had nerve damage, and she had lost most of her deep tendon reflexes. The clincher was the presence of Aldrich-Mees lines on Carol's toenails and fingernails. This is a clear indicator of arsenic poisoning.

With the probable cause of Carol's illness now isolated, doctors sought confirmation by sending samples of her hair for testing. These revealed 50 times the normal level of arsenic. And since there was no indication as to how Carol might accidentally have ingested such a high amount of the toxin, the hospital called in the police. Their independent tests, conducted by the Alabama Department of Forensic Sciences, showed results consistent with the poison being administered in ever increasing amounts over a period of four to eight months. During the course of this investigation, the police also learned of the untimely death of Frank Hilley, who had suffered symptoms that were remarkably similar to those of his daughter.

Frank Hilley's body was exhumed for testing on October 3, 1979, with analysis showing 10 times the normal level of arsenic in hair samples and 100 times the normal level in the toenails. The conclusion was that Frank had been deliberately given arsenic over a number of months and that the toxicity in his body had gradually increased to the level where it had killed him. He'd died a protracted and painful death.

Of course, there was an obvious link between the two poisoning victims, Frank and Carol. That link was Marie Hilley, who had benefited financially from Frank's death and would have received another payday had Carol's illness run its course. Ironically, Marie was in the county lockup at that time, awaiting trial for fraud charges relating to bad checks. Now she had a far more serious indictment to answer. On October 9, 1979, she was charged with the attempted murder of her daughter. A subsequent search turned up a vial in her purse which was tested and found to contain traces of arsenic. Investigators believed that she had obtained the lethal substance from a commercially available brand of rat poison.

At this point, Marie had still not yet been indicted for Frank's murder. On November 9, she was released on bond of just $10,000 and promptly disappeared. A note left at a local motel, where she had been staying, indicated that she'd been kidnapped, but the police weren't buying that obvious ruse. She was listed as a fugitive from justice, and a warrant was issued for her immediate arrest.

On November 19, there was a break-in at the home of one of Marie's aunts. Items of women's clothing and an overnight bag were taken, and the family's car was also missing. A note left by the perpetrator warned the family not to inform the police or "we will burn you out." But investigators had little doubt as to who might have written the threatening message. And with a description of the car that Marie was driving and the clothes that she was likely to be wearing, they were confident that they would make a quick arrest. Unfortunately, they had vastly underestimated Marie Hilley's criminal cunning. She would prove to be a very slippery customer indeed.

By the turn of the year, with Marie still at large, the FBI was called into the investigation. Yet, despite the Bureau's vast resources, despite a massive, multi-state manhunt, there was no sign of the fugitive. On January 11, 1980, the search became even more urgent when Marie was indicted (in absentia) for the murder of her husband. In the interim, the authorities had carried out two more exhumations – of Marie's mother, Lucille Frazier, and her mother-in-law, Carrie Hilley. Both women were found to have elevated levels of arsenic in their bodies, although the amounts were not considered fatal.

But where was Marie while all of this was going on? After fleeing Alabama, she'd traveled to Florida, where she assumed a new identity, calling herself Robbi Hannon. In May of 1980, she met a man named John Homan, who she subsequently married, taking his last name. In 1981, she and Homan moved to New Hampshire. During this time, Marie spoke frequently of her imaginary twin sister, "Teri", who supposedly lived in Texas. Given what happened next, it is clear that she was laying the ground for yet another of her outrageous deceptions.

In the summer of 1982, Marie informed her husband that she needed to take a trip to Texas to attend to some family business and also to see doctors about an undisclosed illness. Homan was reluctant for her to make the journey alone, especially if she was ill, but Marie insisted. She left in August 1982 and traveled to Texas and Florida, now using the alias Teri Martin. About a month later, she called John Homan from Texas, identifying herself as Teri Martin, his wife's twin sister. She told him that "Robbi" had died but that there was no need for him to come to Texas since there would not be a funeral. Robbi's remains had been donated to medical science.

One can only assume the impact that this devastating news must have had on John Homan. But Marie wasn't done with him just yet. On November 13, 1980, she showed up in New Hampshire with a new hairstyle and hair color and having lost a considerable amount of weight. She introduced herself as Teri Martin, the twin of his "deceased" wife. Amazingly, Homan bought the deception.

Soon after Marie's return to New Hampshire, John Homan placed an obituary to his dead wife in the Keene Sentinel, a local newspaper. Then, on Marie's insistence, he took her to her "sister's" former place of employment, where she introduced herself to Robbi's former colleagues as Teri, the twin sister they'd heard so much about. It was another brilliant piece of acting on Marie's part, but not everyone was convinced. Speculation as to the true identity of the surprise visitor would continue for months, until someone eventually contacted the New Hampshire state police and reported their suspicions.

A covert inquiry was launched, leading investigators to the conclusion that "Robbi Homan" was indeed posing as her own twin, possibly as a means to pull off an insurance scam. Marie had, in the meanwhile, found a job and had settled down to life with John Homan, telling him that they could provide comfort to one another while they were "getting over Robbi's death." The police pulled her in for questioning in January 1983. During that interrogation, she stunned investigators by admitting that she was not Teri Martin. She was not even Robbi Homan but Audrey Marie Hilley, currently a fugitive from justice and a murder suspect in Alabama.

Marie Hilley was returned to Alabama on January 19, 1983. With her bail set at $320,000, she would spend the time leading up to her trial behind bars. But at least she had the love of her family to see her through. Even Carol, the daughter she'd tried to murder, forgave her. So, too, did John Homan. Despite the horrible deception that Marie had pulled on him, he moved to Anniston to be close to her.

Audrey Marie Hilley was brought to trial in June 1983. The case against her was overwhelming, and despite Carol testifying that she did not believe her mother had tried to kill her, the jury took just three hours to return its verdict. Marie Hilley was found guilty of the murder of Frank Hilley and of the attempted murder of Carol Hilley. The following day, she received a life sentence for murder and twenty years for the attempted murder.

Marie was transferred to Tutwiler State Women's Prison in Wetumpka, Alabama, to begin her sentence. There, she proved to be a model prisoner and was reclassified within two years as a minimum security inmate. That meant that she qualified for periodic furloughs. The first of those, an eight-hour pass, was granted in late 1986.

But the authorities had still not learned their lesson with Marie Hilley. Marie was a runner who would never accept her incarceration, no matter how cushy the conditions. Three furloughs came and went without incident. Then, on February, 19, 1987, Marie left on a three-day pass and never returned.

During her previous flight from justice, Hilley had remained at large for nigh on three years, assuming various aliases. The authorities fully expected that she'd pull off another successful escape and that it would take a long and arduous search to bring her back. They were wrong.

On the wet and cold evening of February 26, a 911 call brought police and emergency services to a house on the outskirts of Blue Mountain, Alabama. The householder, Susan Craft, explained that a delirious woman had shown up on her porch, saying she needed help. The woman said that her name was Sellers and that her car had broken down nearby, but given her disheveled appearance, Craft suspected that she was lying. She nonetheless invited the woman inside to wait while she called a tow truck. That was when the woman collapsed on the porch and started convulsing. Craft then ran inside and called 911.

Marie Hilley had spent four days wandering the woods between Anniston and Blue Mountain, sleeping outdoors without shelter or warm clothing, in wet and frigid conditions. By the time she collapsed on Sue Craft's porch, she was suffering from acute hypothermia. She was still alive when paramedics arrived but soon lapsed into unconsciousness. She died of heart failure on the way to the hospital. Marie was laid to rest by her children on February 28, 1987. The grave that she occupies is beside Frank Hilley, the husband she'd murdered.

Melissa Ann Friedrich

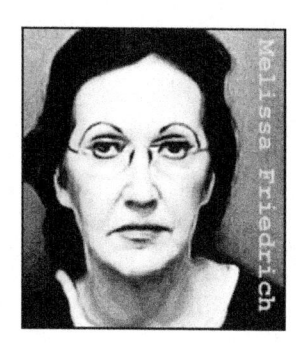

Black widows and Bluebeards are generally considered to be financially motivated killers. Their M.O. is usually to dupe unsuspecting victims into marrying them (often bigamously) and then getting them to sign over everything they own. Once that is achieved the victim is swiftly dispatched before the killer moves on to the next "project." However, most of these killers have a motive that goes beyond money. They enjoy the thrill of the hunt, entangling the victim in a web of lies, watching as they hurtle unknowingly towards their doom. It is akin to playing God.

Melissa Ann Stewart was born in Burnt Church, New Brunswick, on May 16, 1938. As a teen, she moved with her family to Ontario where, in 1955, she met and married factory worker Russell Sheppard. Melissa was just 17 at the time, but she left her family behind to move with her new husband to his hometown of Montague, Prince Edward Island. By the age of 20, she was mother to two children, a boy and a girl. She had also run afoul of the law for the first time, racking up an 11-month jail term for forgery. She would spend one-third of the next 15 years behind bars on various fraud and forgery charges.

Needless to say, Melissa's propensity for petty crime put a strain on her marriage, and the couple separated. In 1988, she moved in with widower Gordon Stewart, later marrying him in twin ceremonies in Las Vegas and Vancouver. Unbeknownst to Stewart, the marriage was invalid. His bride was still married to her first husband and wouldn't obtain a divorce until May 1991.

And that wasn't all that Gordon Stewart didn't know about his new wife. The couple had barely set up house in Vancouver, British Columbia, when money started to go missing from Gordon's bank accounts. At around the same time, Melissa started accusing her husband of sexual and physical abuse.

Just before Christmas 1990, Gordon Stewart was admitted to a Vancouver Hospital. He appeared disoriented and was foaming at the mouth. Doctors soon discovered why. He had ingested large amounts of benzodiazepine, a psychoactive drug usually prescribed for insomnia or anxiety. Stewart swore that he hadn't taken the drug, but doctors didn't believe him. He would, in any case, make a full recovery and so the matter went no further.

A couple of months later, police officers were called to a domestic disturbance at the Stewart home. After a cursory investigation, Gordon was arrested for assault. A guilty plea to the charge saw him spend three weeks in jail. By the time he was released in March 1991, Gordon found that Melissa had obtained a restraining order against him. Defying that order, he tracked Melissa down and begged her to take him back. Eventually, she agreed, and in April the couple moved together to Dartmouth, Nova Scotia. Their reconciliation would not last long.

On April 27, 1991, a distraught Melissa called the Dartmouth police to report an accident. She said that she and her husband had been driving near Halifax Airport when they'd gotten into an argument. Melissa had been at the wheel and Gordon had demanded that she stop so that he could get out. She had done as he asked, but just as she was pulling off, he'd jumped in front of the car and she had "accidentally" struck him. Afraid of what he might do to her, she had not stopped, instead driving home to report the accident.

Officers quickly responded to the scene and found Gordon Stewart exactly where Melissa had said he'd be. But that was the only piece of information she'd given accurately. Gordon was dead, and it was clear that he had been hit more than once. An autopsy would also find alcohol and benzodiazepine in his system, suggesting that he had probably been passed out at the time Melissa dragged him from the vehicle and then rode over him. Soon the police had tracked down two eyewitnesses who could back up their theory. They'd seen Marie drive over her husband, back up, and then drive over him again. The timeline also suggested that she'd waited three hours before calling the police.

Melissa was charged with murder. At her trial, she sobbingly admitted to killing Gordon but said that it had been the culmination of years of abuse, during which she'd frequently been beaten, raped, and sodomized. It was a convincing performance, and it swayed the jury who found her not guilty of murder but guilty of manslaughter. Melissa was sentenced to six years in prison. She served just two.

As the new century dawned, Melissa Stewart was a woman in her early 60s, still fairly attractive and still keen on male companionship despite her earlier experiences. She'd also found a new way of meeting potential partners – the Internet. She began scouting dating sites, paying particular attention to Christian pages aimed at seniors. It was through this medium that she came across retired engineer Robert Friedrich in April 2000. The two began corresponding, and a month later Friedrich invited her to visit him at his home in Florida. At their first meeting, she told him flat-out that she believed God wanted them to be together. Within three days, they were talking wedding plans. A month later, they were married in Dartmouth, Nova Scotia. Thereafter Melissa relocated to Bradenton, Florida, to live with her new husband.

It wasn't long after the wedding before Robert Friedrich's family began noticing changes in his behavior. His health deteriorated and his speech became slurred. The family suspected that Melissa was responsible, and in July 2002, one of Friedrich's sons even lodged a complaint with the Elder Abuse Line. Six months later, Friedrich was dead of an apparent heart attack. During the two years of his marriage to Melissa, he had made her the sole beneficiary of his $100,000 estate.

Unsurprisingly, Robert Friedrich's family was highly suspicious of the circumstances under which he died. They complained to the county sheriff, alleging that Melissa had poisoned him. Unfortunately, as the body had been cremated, there was no way of proving this. Melissa stayed on in Florida for the next two years where she continued to cash her husband's Social Security checks. In the interim, a civil suit had stripped her of all but $15,000 of Robert Friedrich's estate.

Melissa returned to Canada in 2004, but by the end of the year, she was back in Florida, pursuing another man who she'd met online, 73-year-old Alex Strategos. On the night of their very first date, she followed him back to his Pinellas Park apartment and announced that she was moving in. A familiar pattern soon followed. Strategos began suffering dizzy spells, slurred speech, and small accidents. Over the next three months, he was taken to the ER on no fewer than eight occasions. During one of those visits, Melissa persuaded him to give her power of attorney over his financial affairs. She then began siphoning money out of his accounts.

Fortunately, Alex Strategos's son was not taken in by Melissa's slick line of talk. After he noticed that benzodiazepine had shown up on his father's blood tests and saw that there were several large withdrawals from his father's bank account, Dean Strategos went to the police. On January 6, 2005, Melissa Friedrich was arrested and charged with grand theft, fraud, and forgery. She accepted a plea bargain and was sentenced to five years in prison.

In 2009, Melissa was released from a Florida jail and deported to Canada. She moved into a senior's complex in Nova Scotia. Yet even now, at the age of 74, she wasn't done. She was soon trawling the dating websites looking for another meal ticket. She found one in 75-year-old Fred Weeks.

Weeks married Melissa on September 25, 2012, but he barely made it past the honeymoon. After traveling to a guesthouse in North Sydney, Nova Scotia, on September 28, the couple retired to their room. The following morning, Melissa advised the staff that her husband was ill and needed an ambulance. However, she insisted on finishing her breakfast before the ambulance was called. Paramedics found a frail and disorientated Fred Weeks lying on the floor of the couple's room. He was rushed to hospital where tests showed a high dose of benzodiazepine in his body.

Fred Weeks would eventually make a full recovery. But that did not mean that Melissa was off the hook. A search of the Weeks household had turned up a large stash of prescription drugs, including 144 Lorazepam, prescribed to Melissa by five different doctors. This saw her charged with the attempted murder of Fred Weeks, but again she struck a deal, accepting a prison term of three years. She walked free from that term in 2016. Both the American and Canadian authorities are currently investigating her for Social Security fraud amounting to tens of thousands of dollars.

Dorothea Waddingham

Few murderers divide opinion quite as much as Dorothea Nancy Waddingham. On the one hand, there are those who describe her as a heartless murder-for-profit killer who killed two sickly women entrusted to her care. On the other hand, there are those who insist that Waddingham did not commit her crimes out of greed, but rather out of desperation. She desperately wanted a better life for herself and her five children; she was forced into a corner by her ailing business; the two women she killed were given a peaceful end to their terrible suffering. That Waddingham was a murderer is not in doubt. She confessed as much before going to the gallows. But which was she, callous fiend or angel of mercy? You decide.

Dorothea Waddingham was born in 1899 on a farm at Hucknall, just outside of Nottingham, England. Her family was reasonably well off, and she was allowed to finish school before taking up a job at a factory. Thereafter, she found work as a ward maid at the Burton-on-Trent Workhouse infirmary. That short stint constituted the full extent of her "medical training."

In 1925, Dorothea met and married a man named Willoughby Leech, who at 52 was twice her age. Leech was also dying of cancer, but during the eight years they were together, he fathered three children by Dorothea. During that time, Dorothea served two short prison terms, one for fraud and another for theft. She was also forced to resign her job at the infirmary over the theft of toothbrushes.

Willoughby Leech finally succumbed to his disease in 1933, and thereafter Dorothea reverted to her maiden name. She had by then already started a relationship with the lodger in their home, a man named Ronald Joseph Sullivan. He was thirteen years older than her, but the relationship appeared to be a happy one. Over its course, Dorothea bore two more children, and with their growing family, she and Sullivan sought out bigger premises. That brought them to the large house at number 32, Devon Drive, Nottingham. It was here that either Waddingham or Sullivan hit on the idea of opening a nursing home.

Neither, of course, had the necessary qualifications. However, such was the desperate need for care facilities that the county authorities granted them a license. Soon after, they took in four patients, all aged and infirm, three of whom died within months. The remaining resident, a Mrs. Kemp, was in great pain from gangrene and Parkinson's disease. She was being prescribed large doses of morphine, which the doctor, H.H. Mansfield, allowed Waddingham to administer, even though she wasn't qualified to do so.

On January 12, 1935, the County Nursing Association referred two new patients, 89-year-old Louisa Baguley, and her daughter Ada who was fifty years old. Ada was afflicted by a progressive disease that left her unable to walk. The fee for these two patients was thirty shillings (£1.50) a week, a pittance given the long hours put into caring for them.

In February, the number of patients was reduced to two when Mrs. Kemp died. Waddingham was now running the nursing home and supporting her large family on a wholly inadequate thirty shillings per week.

Relief was soon at hand, though. On May 6, 1935, the elder Mrs. Baguley rewrote her will, leaving her entire estate to Dorothea Waddingham on the condition that Waddingham would continue to care for her and her daughter until their deaths. The estate was worth around £1,600, a considerable sum of money for the time. Five days later, Mrs. Baguley died. Based on Waddingham's description of her symptoms, Dr. Mansfield listed cause of death as 'cerebral hemorrhage.'

Her mother's death threw Ada Baguley into a deep depression. Dr. Mansfield increased her medication, but her condition continued to worsen through the summer months. In September 1935, an old family friend, Alice Briggs, came to visit Ada, which at least cheered her up. Mrs. Briggs even told Waddingham (with Ada nodding enthusiastically in the background) that she was going to bring Ada to her house for tea in a couple of days time.

But just a day after that visit, on September 11, Ronald Sullivan called Dr. Mansfield and told him that Ada had lapsed into a coma. By the time Mansfield arrived at the home, Ada was dead. As death had been expected at any time, Dr. Mansfield was not in the least bit suspicious. He filled out the death certificate stating that Ada had died of cardiovascular degeneration.

With Ada gone, Dorothea Waddingham stood to become a rather wealthy woman. But here it all began to go wrong for her. According to Waddingham, Ada had asked to be cremated and had also insisted that her family should not be informed of her death. This second request seemed strange, but Waddingham produced a letter, written by Sullivan and signed by Ada, to back up her claim. That only increased suspicion. Then there was the issue of the cremation. That could only go ahead with the approval of Ada's family. Pressed on the matter, Waddingham insisted that Ada had no family. This, of course, was a lie, and would come back to haunt Waddingham at her trial.

The cremation, meanwhile, had been referred to the 'Cremation Referee,' Dr. Cyril Black, who was also the Medical Officer of Health in Nottingham. Black had strong opinions on nursing homes run by non-medical personnel and was particularly scathing in his assessment of Waddingham's facility. After reading the note that Ada Baguley had signed, he instructed that a postmortem must be performed before the cremation could take place.

The postmortem found no evidence that Ada had died of cardiovascular degeneration. Indeed, the examining physician, Dr. Taylor, stated that she could have lived a few more years, at least. The true cause of death was to be found in the stomach, liver, and kidneys, where Taylor detected over three grains of morphine, certainly enough to have killed her.

With foul play now suspected in the death of Ada Baguley, an order was granted for her mother's remains to be exhumed. She, too, was found to have died from morphine poisoning. In short order, Dorothea Waddingham and Ronald Sullivan found themselves under arrest and charged with two counts of murder.

The trial of Waddingham and Sullivan was one of the most sensational of the era. It began at the Nottingham Assizes on February 4, 1936, before Justice Rayner Goddard. Despite the fact that Ronald Sullivan had written the letter that had first roused suspicion against the couple, the judge ruled that there was insufficient evidence against him and dismissed the charges. Dorothea was left to face trial on her own.

And she almost immediately got herself into trouble when she admitted giving morphine to the Baguleys. She insisted, however, that she had done so on Dr. Mansfield's instructions. It only took the doctor to take the stand and deny her claim for her to be exposed in a lie. The morphine, he testified, had most likely come from the medication he'd prescribed for Mrs. Kemp.

As the evidence continued to mount against Waddingham, it became clear to all present that there was only likely to be one outcome. Yet even though the jury returned a guilty verdict on February 27, they did so with a recommendation of mercy. Ignoring their advice, Judge Goddard donned the black cap and sentenced Dorothea Waddingham to death.

Waddingham was taken to Winson Green prison in Birmingham to await her fate. Thereafter followed a desperate round of appeals to save her life. Public opinion was firmly behind the disgraced caregiver, but the Home Secretary refused to budge. Her last appeal denied, Dorothea Waddingham went to the gallows on April 16, 1936. She died while 10,000 protesters gathered outside the prison on her behalf. It would later be revealed that she had confessed on the scaffold that she'd deliberately killed Louisa and Ada Baguley.

Inessa Tarverdiyeva

Inessa Tarverdiyeva was a nursery school teacher. Her husband, Roman Podkopaev, was a former paratrooper with an elite unit of the Russian army. He was also a qualified dentist. The couple lived a comfortable middle-class existence in Stavropol, a picturesque city in the southwest of Russia, sharing their home with their 13-year-old daughter, Anastasiya, and with Inessa's 25-year-old daughter from her previous marriage, Viktoria. To neighbors, they seemed a normal, happy family who loved the outdoors and enjoyed camping. That, in fact, was exactly what the family wanted them to believe. Behind the façade of middle-class mediocrity lay a deep, dark secret.

Beginning in the year 2008, the area around Rostov-on-Don began experiencing a steep increase in violent crime. It started on the night of February 17 when someone broke into the home of Mikhail Zlydnev and brutally murdered him and his wife. The Zlydnevs were first shot, then finished off in a frenzied knife attack which a police official later described as a "bloodbath." Very little was taken from the well-appointed home, leaving the police to conclude that the murders might have been committed by drug dealers. Mikhail Zlydnev had been a security head at a state drug enforcement agency.

Five months later, on July 17, 2008, a couple was driving along the federal highway near Aksay when their vehicle came under small arms fire from the roadside. Alexei Sazonov and Julia Vasilyeva died at the scene. Their bullet-riddled bodies were found soon after. Given that all cash and valuables had been removed from the car, the police put the crime down to bandits and made no connection to the Zlydnev murders.

They were wrong in that assumption, of course. The murders were connected. In fact, they had a common set of perpetrators and those perpetrators were neither drug dealers nor road bandits but a supposedly law-abiding family from Stavropol.

Almost a year passed. Then, on July 8, 2009, Colonel Dmitry Chudakov was driving with his family back to his home in the town of Nizhny Novgorod. At some point during the journey, Chudakov decided to take a break and pulled over to the side of the road. That simple act turned out to be a deadly mistake. No sooner had he brought his vehicle to a stop when they came under fire. The colonel and his 7-year-old son were killed in the initial barrage while his wife and daughter, on the other side of the car, ducked for cover. But their respite would be brief. They were pulled from the vehicle and knifed to death at the roadside, 11-year-old daughter, Veronika, suffering 37 savage wounds. The killers then ransacked the family's luggage, stealing a laptop computer, a hairdryer, and a camera, although curiously leaving behind items of gold jewelry.

The murder of a high-ranking military officer and the massacre of his family caused a furor that went well beyond the Nizhny Novgorod Oblast. Pressure was applied to the police, and they responded within days by making an arrest. The main evidence against the man they arrested was ballistics. Bullets from the crime scene had been linked to a weapon that he supposedly owned. Despite protesting his innocence, Alexei Serenko was denied bail and sent to jail awaiting trial. He would remain there for nearly two years before the police admitted their mistake. By then, investigators had connected the three unsolved massacres via ballistics, although they still had no idea who was responsible.

And they'd soon have more names to add to the burgeoning list of victims. On March 10, 2009, Inessa Tarverdiyeva and her family of killers invaded a home on the outskirts of Novocherkassk, murdered the two residents, and made off with a laptop, a camera, and various items of clothing. They followed that up with a particularly brutal double homicide, even by their standards. Believing that a certain residence contained cash and firearms, they broke in and waited for the family to return. When the two teenaged daughters came home alone, they ambushed them, tied them up and then started torturing them to find out the location of the loot. The girls had their eyes gouged out before they were put out of their suffering. One of the victims was later revealed to be Inessa Tarverdiyeva's god-daughter.

And still the carnage continued. On September 19, 2012, the family broke into a dental clinic in Novocherkassk, triggering a silent alarm in the process. When security guards Vladimir Mandrik and Vasily Camforin responded, they were ruthlessly gunned down. On November 29, 2012, taxi driver Vadim Lozhkov was killed in his home. The murder weapon turned out to be a Kalashnikov stolen from one of the security guards. On March 16, 2013, Nikolai Kutsekon heard his car alarm go off and went to investigate. He was gunned down in the street. On April 8, 2013, two grocery store employees were shot after responding to an alarm. Nikolai Korsunov survived, but Yuri Statsenko died on the way to hospital. Again, ballistics would link this crime to the others in the series.

Sixteen people were now dead, and still the police did not have a clue as to who was responsible. The press, however, had given the perpetrators a moniker that did nothing to still the anxiety of Rostovites. At one of the crime scenes, the police had picked up a dagger with the words "My favorite Amazon" inscribed on the blade. Thus, the press started referring to the "Gang of Amazons," a descriptor that led the general public to perceive the killers as female. This was given credence when sole survivor, Nikolai Korsunov, told the police that one of the shooters in the grocery store heist had been a woman. (Incidentally, the dagger found at the crime scene turned out to have nothing to do with the murders.)

On April 24, 2013, the "Gang of Amazons" struck again, this time in the Aksay district. Police lieutenant Andrei Yurin was returning home late at night when he was ambushed outside his home and shot to death. The gang then tried to force their way into his residence but were thwarted by the security system and fled empty-handed. That undoubtedly saved the lives of Yurin's wife and baby daughter.

But Inessa and her gang had erred badly in murdering a police officer. Up until now, the police had come in for a lot of criticism for their failure to catch the killers. Much of that criticism was unfair, but some of it was valid. The response generated by the murder of Andrei Yurin proved that they certainly could have been doing more. Now the investigation escalated significantly, with road blocks and additional patrols. On September 8, 2013, one of those patrols paid off.

Roman Podkopaev and his stepdaughter Viktoria had gone out alone that night, riding a scooter as they trawled for victims in and around Aksay. They soon found a couple, strolling hand-in-hand through a park, and executed them. Then they staged a home invasion at the residence of a former military officer, killing the man without remorse. Finding no cash or valuables, they proceeded to loot the victim's refrigerator and liquor cabinet before setting off for home clutching their grocery bags of loot. They had traveled only a short distance when they encountered a police patrol.

Podkopaev and Viktoria were ordered from their scooter and told to produce ID. Instead, Podkopaev reached into his coat and brought out a pistol. His first shot, fired at point blank range, hit officer Ivan Shakhovoi in the face and killed him on the spot. Podkopaev then tried to flee but was cut down by a hail of bullets. He died at the scene. Viktoria, caught in the crossfire, was seriously injured but would survive.

It did not take the police long to link the two gang members to Inessa Tarverdiyeva who was at a local campsite with her daughter Anastasiya awaiting their return. Found in her possession was a large cache of weapons, including 20 firearms, silencers, hand grenades, and boxes of ammunition. A later search of the family home, back in Stavropol, would turn up items stolen from their many victims.

Inessa Tarverdiyeva showed little remorse for the thirty-plus murders that her family had committed. Indeed, she seemed to regard herself as some sort of folk-hero, akin to Robin Hood. "I am a gangster by nature," she proudly stated. She also professed to a deep-seated hatred of the police. When she heard that her husband had killed one officer and wounded another, her response was: "It is a pity that he did not kill them very much."

Inessa was also quite forthcoming about the gang's methodology, describing it as "a day at the office." They would use their frequent camping trips as cover for the crimes they committed. Their favorite hunting ground was the Don River basin, including the town of Rostov and its surrounds. This was an 18-hour drive from their home, but the family would make the journey, set up at one of the many campsites in the area, and use that as a base of operations. From there, they would spread out into the surrounding area, scouting for victims of opportunity while staying in communication by walkie-talkie. Anyone who attracted their interest was as good as dead.

Much debate in the press at the time centered on whether Inessa or her husband was the leader of the gang. Inessa was ambivalent on the issue. All she would say was that she only killed adults and that all of the children had been killed by Roman. Nonetheless, Roman was dead, and it was Inessa and Viktoria who would face the full force of the law.

That would turn out to be a prison term of just 21 years in Inessa's case and 19 years for Viktoria. Russian courts are generally lenient towards female offenders. Anastasiya, as a minor, was given a nominal juvenile sentence.

Debora Green

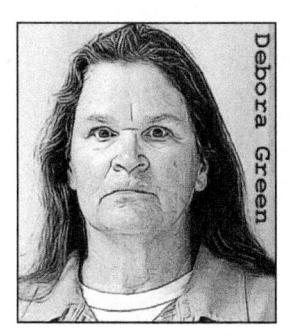

If ever there was anyone who personified the American dream, it was Debora Jones. Born to a delivery truck driver and a homemaker on February 28, 1951, Debora showed signs of her unusual intellect from early childhood. By the age of three, she had already learned how to read and write, putting her well ahead of her peers when she started school. She'd later master a second language and learn to play a musical instrument; she'd become a National Merit Scholar; when she graduated, it was as valedictorian of her high school class. In short, Debora's early life was one of near unbroken success.

And that success showed no sign of waning when Debora entered the University of Illinois in the fall of 1969. Her major was chemistry and, as with all else, she excelled at it, graduating in 1972. Her intention had been to pursue a career as a chemical engineer. But with diploma in hand and a seemingly promising future ahead of her, Debora made a fateful decision. She decided that her career prospects as an engineer would be limited and that a vocation in medicine offered better opportunities. Soon after, she registered at the University of Kansas School of Medicine, remaining there until graduation in 1975. Her specialty was emergency medicine, and she was quickly snapped up by the Truman Medical Center to work in its Emergency Room.

By then, Debora was already a married woman, having wed her longtime boyfriend, Duane Green, while studying at the University of Kansas. Life should have been perfect. But already, Debora was having misgivings about her chosen career path. The very things that made her a talented engineer made her a poor emergency doctor. She enjoyed sifting through reams of data to solve complex problems. In the pressure cooker environment of the ER, where decisions had to be made on the fly and carried life and death implications, she faltered. She became short-tempered with colleagues and patients, and that irritability often carried over into her home life. She and Duane Green divorced in 1978. She said that they had little in common. He said that she was cold and uncaring.

Those who had known Debora Green up to that point described her as a supremely confident woman. But that confidence had been built on years of continuous success, and with the failure of her marriage and a faltering career, the first cracks were beginning to appear. Green tried to arrest those setbacks by switching from emergency medicine to oncology, but she found that the high death rate among her cancer patients upset her emotionally.

There was, at least, some respite on the relationship front. Debora had begun dating Michael Farrar, a final year medical student who was four years her junior. Attracted by Green's sharp intellect and seemingly boundless energy, Farrar was nonetheless concerned about her explosive and unpredictable temper. He put it down to the stresses of her job. The couple was married on May 26, 1979. For some reason,

Debora opted to continue using her previous married name, Green. Shortly after the wedding, Farrar accepted a residency at the University of Cincinnati, and the couple moved to Ohio where Debora found work at Jewish Hospital, back in the ER.

By the early 1980s, the Farrars were settled in Cincinnati, Ohio. Debora, by now, was showing increasing signs of instability, mostly manifest in her growing hypochondria. She began suffering from migraines, muscular pains, and insomnia, and started abusing prescription medications. Despite this, she became pregnant with her first child. Timothy was born on January 20, 1982.

Debora initially appeared delighted at the new arrival. But within six weeks, she'd apparently become bored with the idea and decided to go back to work. Hiring a nanny to look after Timothy, she registered for a course in hematology at the University of Cincinnati. Two years later, a second child, Kate, was born. Again Debora was back at her studies within six weeks.

But the former golden girl and academic colossus was about to suffer yet another blow to her ego. Plagued by headaches and increasingly reliant on medication to help her cope, she failed her exams. In the meanwhile, her husband's career was flourishing. He was offered a position in Kansas City, Missouri, and the family relocated there. Debora, in the unfamiliar role of no longer being the family's main breadwinner, soon found work at a medical practice. But her offhanded manner towards her patients caused friction with the other doctors, and she was not offered a hoped-for partnership. Angry and humiliated, she set up her own practice. Then, just as the business was beginning to gain traction, she became pregnant with her third child, Kelly, born on December 13, 1988.

Debora again took only six weeks maternity leave before returning to work. She was determined to get her practice up and running again, if only to restore her waning self-confidence. But her short time away had been a mortal blow to the fledgling business. Patient numbers had dropped off significantly and would never recover. Reluctantly, Debora was forced to close the practice. Disgusted, she decided to abandon her medical career altogether and become a stay-at-home mom. By now, she was 50 pounds overweight and suffering near-constant back pain. She often appeared intoxicated, with slurred speech and unsteadiness due to her overreliance on sedatives. When confronted by her husband, she agreed to stop self-medicating or, at least, to cut back. For a while, at least, she seemed to do just that.

The Farrar children were all active outside the home. Timothy played soccer and ice hockey, while Kate was a promising ballerina who was dancing with the Missouri State Ballet by the age of ten. While her husband, Mike, worked long hours at his medical practice, Debora could be found ferrying her children to and from their various extra-curricular activities. Some regarded her as a good mother who doted on her kids. Others felt that she pushed her children too hard and publicly criticized them if they didn't live up to her standards.

Inside the Farrar home, the situation was even more fractious. Debora and Mike were constantly at each other's throats. He accused her of being a poor housekeeper (which she was, the house was always in a mess, and she never cooked, sustaining herself and her children on an unhealthy diet of takeaway meals). He also blamed her for turning the children against him (which was also true). Debora fought back by accusing him of having affairs. Inevitably, all of this accusation and counteraccusation led to a breakdown of the marriage. In January 1994, Mike asked for a divorce, triggering a furious response from Debora. She attacked him physically, screaming and throwing objects. The next day, he moved out of the family home. The couple attempted a reconciliation four months later, but it was clear that it wasn't going to work. Mike soon moved back into an apartment.

A short while later, a fire broke out at the Farrar family home, rendering it uninhabitable and the family effectively homeless. This forced Mike Farrar into a situation again where he had to cohabitate with his estranged wife, first at his apartment, then in a home that he purchased for the family at Prairie Village.

That move appeared to bring about a change in Debora's behavior. She pledged to change her ways, and for a while, she did. She began cooking and cleaning for the family and appeared altogether more congenial. But of course, it couldn't last. In the summer of 1995, the family departed for a vacation in Peru. On their return, Mike again broached the subject of divorce with Debora. She responded as she had before, violently and hysterically.

An uneasy truce now ensued. Mike had since become involved in a relationship with another woman, but he refused to move out and leave his children in Debora's care. She had begun drinking heavily while continuing to abuse prescription drugs. Despite her inebriated state, she still insisted on driving the children to after-school activities. In the evenings, she would drink herself to the point of unconsciousness. And she was an abusive drunk, staggering around the apartment and aiming foul-mouthed rants at her husband and children. Yet despite her unpredictable behavior, despite her colorful language and explosive outbursts, Mike Farrar was certain of one thing. He was certain that Debora would never deliberately harm the children.

One day, while Mike was sitting in front of the TV, Debora brought him a sandwich. This was unusual, but Mike had become accustomed to his wife's unpredictable behavior. He was glad, anyway, of a temporary truce, so he thanked her and bit into the sandwich. It tasted slightly bitter. Later that night, Mike began to feel nauseous and only just made it to the bathroom in time to throw up into the bowl. Soon he was overcome by vomiting, diarrhea, and dizziness. That same evening, he was rushed to the hospital where he would spend a week recovering. Doctors believed that he might have picked up a bug in Peru, but by the time he was discharged, he appeared to have recovered fully. That was until he consumed another meal prepared by Debora. Then his symptoms returned with a vengeance. Soon he was back in the hospital again.

Mike's friends were convinced that Debora was trying to kill him, but he refused to believe that she would do such a thing. He was, however, curious enough to search her handbag while she was out. There he found a sachet of castor beans from which the deadly poison ricin is derived. When he confronted Debora with the evidence, she said that she had bought the beans in order to kill herself, that she'd rather die than lose him to another woman. It was the last straw. That same evening, Mike Farrar moved out, this time for good.

On Monday, October 23, 1995, Mike spent the afternoon with his children before returning them to the family home at Prairie Village.

He found Debora in a state of inebriation and left quickly, before she could start an argument. Later that evening, he received several drunken and abusive calls from his estranged wife. Eventually, he retired to bed only to be woken in the early morning hours of October 24 and told that his family home was on fire. He immediately dressed and rushed to the scene.

The story would later emerge that Debora had woken a neighbor just after midnight to say that her house was on fire. She appeared dazed, divorced from the seriousness of the situation. The neighbor immediately called 911. When the first firefighters arrived on the scene at around 12:27, they found Debora and her middle daughter, ten-year-old Kate, standing outside the burning house. Kate begged firefighters to help her brother and sister, six-year-old Kelly and thirteen-year-old Timothy, who were still trapped inside. Debora, however, said nothing. Witnesses later reported that she appeared "very calm, very cool."

The fire was by now raging, and despite their efforts, firefighters were unable to enter the home. By the time they brought the blaze under control, the house was almost entirely destroyed. The bodies of Tim and Kelly Farrar were not recovered until the next morning. Kelly had died in her bed, most likely of smoke inhalation. Tim's body was found on the ground floor, near the kitchen. He had died in the upstairs corridor while trying to escape the fire, and his body had subsequently fallen through the collapsed upper floor. It was severely burned, with the flesh below the knee entirely seared away.

Debora and Mike, together with their surviving daughter Kate were taken to the Prairie Village police station for questioning. According to

Debora's version of events, she had heard the fire alarm go off but had assumed that it had malfunctioned. While trying to turn it off, she had smelled smoke. She'd then made her way out of the house through the back door and had run to the neighbors for help. When she'd returned, she'd found the house ablaze and her daughter Kate standing on the front lawn. Her husband had by then arrived and had confronted her and asked where the children were. Debora had made no reply but had started crying because she knew that Tim and Kelly were trapped inside.

Detectives were immediately struck by Debora's story. For a mother who had just lost two of her three children, she seemed remarkably unemotional. Indeed, she came across as chatty, almost cheerful. She also seemed to have no problem referring to her children in the past tense and did not once refer to them by name, using instead their ages ("my thirteen-year-old"). Also, investigators wanted to know why she had fled the fire, leaving her children inside the burning house. Debora couldn't provide an answer, but Kate could. She said that her mother had instructed Timothy to stay in his room.

Based on Debora's account and the testimony of Mike and Kate Farrar, the police began to suspect that the fire had been deliberately set. That view was confirmed when the Eastern Kansas Multi-Agency Task Force carried out an arson investigation on the ruined house on October 24. Task force officers discovered clear evidence that an accelerant had been used to start the fire. Their conclusion was that between three and ten gallons of flammable liquid had been poured on the carpets of the ground and second floors, and then set alight. Only one person appeared to have had both the means and the opportunity to carry out the attack.

Debora Green was arrested and charged with arson and two counts of murder on November 22, 1995. She initially pleaded not guilty but later admitted that she'd started the fire while her judgment was impaired due to alcohol consumption. She entered a plea of 'no contest' at her trial and was sentenced to two terms of 40 years in prison. She will be over 80 by the time she becomes eligible for parole.

Anna Zwanziger

Anna Schonleben was born in Nuremberg, Germany, in 1760. Her father was a fairly prosperous innkeeper, but both parents died while Anna was only five years old, and she would spend the next five years shuttling from one reluctant relative to the next. In 1770, fate finally smiled on the young girl when she was taken in by a wealthy sponsor. This new benefactor provided her with a good education, and she grew to be a pretty and bright young lady. All the more surprising, then, that her guardian married her off to an alcoholic notary by the name of Zwanziger, twice her age.

Anna's new husband was not cruel to her, merely neglectful. He spent every spare moment in the taverns, leaving her to her own devices. Just 15 years old at the time, Anna assuaged her loneliness by burying herself in books, with a preference for melancholy works. Meanwhile, her husband continued to drink his way through the household budget – and through Anna's inheritance as well. Left in a precarious financial position, Anna was forced into prostitution, although she was picky about her clients, offering herself only to the upper echelons of society. Her husband appeared not to care about these activities as long as they kept him in drink. Nonetheless, a strong bond appears to have existed between them. Anna once left him for a lover, but he pleaded with her to return, and she did. They even divorced on one occasion but were remarried within a day. When Zwanziger died in 1796, Anna appeared distraught. In retrospect, it is by no means certain that she did not have something to do with his demise.

Anna Zwanziger was now 36 years old, and her youthful good looks had long since deserted her. Still, she hoped for a favorable marriage that would restore her to her former station. When no offers were forthcoming, she took up with a former lover, but the man was so cruel to her that she twice attempted suicide. Eventually, she was reduced to earning her living as a housemaid, something she deeply resented. She made a point of ignoring the instructions of her employers and was fired from one job after the other.

In March of 1808, Anna was employed as a housekeeper to an attorney named Glaser who lived at Kasendorf. Glaser was 50 years old, and Anna soon formed the opinion that he was in love with her. She imagined herself the mistress of his household, restored to her former status. It was a picture that pleased her greatly. The only problem was that Glaser was already married, although he'd been estranged from his wife for several years. There and then, Anna formed a devious plan. She wrote letters to the wife, urging her to seek reconciliation. At the same time, she encouraged her employer to make amends with his wife. Within weeks, both parties were convinced, and the couple was reunited.

But the reunion would be a short one. Within a month of Mrs. Glaser returning to her husband, she became gravely ill. By August 26, she was dead. Anna had by now decided that Glaser was not marriage material after all, and within days, she departed the home for a new employer, another lawyer named Grohmann, who lived in nearby Sanspareil.

Grohmann, at twenty-eight, was much younger than Anna's previous employer, although he was severely afflicted by gout. This can be an extremely painful condition, so Grohmann was extremely grateful for Anna's tender and devoted care. She, in turn, began to interpret his gratitude as an unspoken declaration of love. She was devastated when Grohmann announced to his household staff that he was to marry.

A wedding date was set and arrangements made for a grand ball on the estate to celebrate the newlyweds. But as the happy day approached, Grohmann was struck down suddenly by a mysterious illness that left him bed-ridden with diarrhea, vomiting, and severe abdominal pain. The illness lasted eleven days during which Anna never left his side. Grohmann died on May 8, 1809. His death was put down to natural causes due to his long-term health issues. Anna was inconsolable.

Not long after the death of Herr Grohmann, Anna was offered employment in the home of a family named Gebhard. Mrs. Gebhard, who was in the final stages of pregnancy, was particularly pleased to have secured Anna's services as she had heard of the diligence with which she'd nursed her former employer. And she'd bring her special brand of tenderness to the Gebhard household, too. She was even present at the birth of the baby, which went without a hitch.

But just three days after the birth, Mrs. Gebhard was struck down by a mystery ailment, and within a day, she had died in agony. Stepping into the breach as always, Anna took over the care of the infant and nursed it as tenderly as if it were her own. This undoubtedly endeared her to the grieving Herr Gebhard, who praised Anna's qualities as a nursemaid. When friends of the family urged him to get rid of her, calling her a jinx, he flatly refused.

Over the months that followed, a pall seemed to hang over the Gebhard residence. Several of the servants, as well as some visitors, developed minor stomach complaints and bouts of vomiting. No one thought too much of it until September 1, 1809, when Gebhard invited friends around to play skittles and the entire contingent became ill after drinking some beer that Anna had brought up from the cellar. After that incident, Gebhard's friends renewed their pleas, and he eventually agreed to dismiss Anna, although he furnished her with an excellent testimonial.

Anna was deeply hurt by her dismissal and particularly distressed about having to leave the baby in the care of someone else. On the day she was to leave, she was seen filling the saltcellars, something that was not usually part of her duties. Before she left, she prepared hot chocolate for her employer and several of the servants. She also gave the baby a cup of milk.

Within twenty minutes of Anna's departure, everyone who had partaken of her hot chocolate was suffering stomach cramps and vomiting. The baby, too, was ill, although thankfully, she would recover. When some of the servants warned Gebhard against using the salt cellars, saying that they had seen Anna tampering with them, he scolded them for making unfounded allegations. Still, he was suspicious enough to send the containers for chemical analysis. They were all found to be contaminated with arsenic.

And yet, even with clear evidence that Anna had tried to poison his entire household, Gebhard was reluctant to report her to the authorities. He fretted over the issue for a month and was only spurred into action when he received a letter from Anna demanding her job back.

Anna Zwanziger was arrested in October 1809. She initially expressed outrage that anyone would suspect her of being a murderess, but the evidence against her was stacking up pretty quickly. Aside from the arsenic in the saltcellars and the testimony of the servants who had seen her tampering with them, there was forensic proof. Several of her victims had also been exhumed and found to have been poisoned with arsenic.

Confronted with this evidence at her trial in April 1810, Anna collapsed to the floor and suffered an apparent seizure. After she was revived, she stunned the courtroom by confessing. "Arsenic," she said, "has been my truest friend. I killed them all and would have killed more if I'd had the chance."

Anna Zwanziger was publicly beheaded in Nuremburg on September 17, 1811. Before the blade fell, she told her executioners, "It is better for the community that I should die, as it would be impossible for me to stop poisoning people."

Karla Faye Tucker

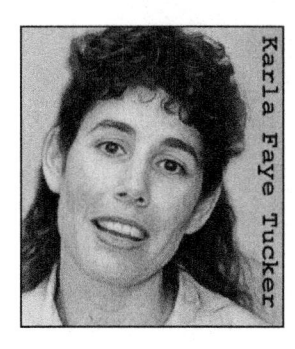

The state of Texas has more death row inmates and executes more prisoners than any other state in the Union. But none of the executions it has carried out has attracted quite as much controversy as that of Karla Faye Tucker in February 1998. For starters, Karla Faye was female, and the Lone Star state had not put a woman to death since the Civil War. Then there was the fact that Karla was under the influence of drugs when she committed the murders she'd been convicted of. There was also no evidence of premeditation, raising doubts as to whether this should even have been a capital case in the first place. It had capital punishment opponents crying foul and calling for the abolition of the death penalty once and for all.

But the law and order lobby also had its say on the Tucker case, and some of the points it raised were difficult to argue against. The petite 24-year-old had committed an extremely savage double homicide, a crime that was touted by many as the most brutal in the state's history. By their reckoning, Karla Faye Tucker fully deserved the sentence that had been handed down to her. A crime of this viciousness could only be repaid with the perpetrator's life.

Karla Faye Tucker was born in Houston, Texas, on November 18, 1959, the youngest of three daughters. Her father, Larry, was a longshoreman who worked the ports along the Texas coastline; her mother, Carolyn, was a homemaker. On the surface, the Tuckers were a happy family. They often vacationed at a cottage they owned on Caney Creek in Brazoria, Texas, and those days would later be remembered by Karla as the happiest of her life. But that happiness was an illusion. Karla's parents had a tempestuous relationship, marred by infidelity and by frequent separations. The couple divorced and remarried several times. Karla would later discover that Larry was not her biological father but that she'd been sired by one of her mother's many lovers. By that time, Larry and Carolyn had split for good, and Karla and her sisters had been packed off to live with their father.

Karla was just 10 years old at the time and was effectively without an adult role model. Larry did his best, but he had a difficult time controlling his three young daughters. At the time, he was working double shifts and was rarely home, leaving the girls to do pretty much as they pleased. And what they chose to do was alarming for girls of such tender years. Karla was just 10 years old when she was introduced to marijuana by her sisters, a mere 11 when she sampled heroin for the first time. A year later, she and her sisters started hanging out with a local motorcycle gang called the Banditos. She was not yet a teenager when she lost her virginity to one of the bikers.

Eventually, it all became too much for Larry Tucker. Unable to control his unruly daughters, he sent them to live with their mother, a move that was never likely to remedy the situation. Carolyn was by then working as a prostitute, and she encouraged her daughters to join her in the trade. By age 14, Karla Faye had dropped out of school and was selling herself on the streets. It was just another step on the downward spiral that would land her, eventually, on death row.

But the road to hell was not a straight one. There were detours *en route.* At age 16, Karla Faye met and married a young man named Stephen Griffith and swore off hooking. Griffith was a hard-drinking mechanic, but he appears to have genuinely loved his wife, appreciating her tough and feisty nature. But like Larry Tucker, he found Karla impossible to control. The marriage was turbulent with the couple fighting often and frequently coming to blows. Despite her diminutive stature, Karla gave as good as she got. Years later, Griffith would recall their time together with misty-eyed affection. "I've never had men hit me as hard as she did. Whenever I went into a bar, I didn't have to worry because I knew that she'd always have my back."

Perhaps predictably, the marriage to Stephen Griffith was a short one. After it broke down, Karla drifted to Houston where she went back to hooking, working the streets of the city's tough Quay Point neighborhood. There, she befriended a woman named Shawn Dean and, through her, was introduced to 37-year-old Danny Garrett, a local dealer. She and Garrett were soon lovers, a convenient situation for Karla since it gave her ready access to drugs. Danny Garrett and Shawn Dean would be key players in the tragic events to come.

On Sunday, June 13, 1983, Karla was at a birthday party for her sister Kari Ann in Houston. This, however, was no ordinary celebration. It had started around midday on Friday and had continued non-stop for three days, fueled by a steady flow of beer, whiskey, and tequila, not to mention valium, mandrax, cocaine, LSD and other drugs. Aside from the narcotic attractions, there was an ongoing sex orgy, sometimes involving one or two couples copulating in full view of other partygoers and at other times involving dozens of celebrants shedding their clothes and their inhibitions to engage in a free-for-all worthy of ancient Rome.

But amidst all of the revelry, there was trouble brewing. Karla's friend, Shawn Dean, had arrived at the party sporting two black eyes and a broken nose, given to her by her estranged husband, Jerry Lynn Dean. Other partygoers sympathized, called Jerry Lynn a scumbag, and told Shawn that her injuries were a small price to pay for freeing herself from him. But not Karla. She was incensed by the beating meted out to her friend, and her anger only grew as the drugs and liquor took hold. Several times during the weekend, she spoke of driving over to Jerry Lynn's apartment and teaching him a lesson. On each occasion, she was dissuaded from doing anything rash. Nonetheless, she continued to vent, and eventually she talked Shawn, Danny Garrett, and another friend, Jimmy Leibrandt, around to her way of thinking. Danny, however, was adamant that she should not go to Jerry Lynn's place without him.

At around 7 o'clock on that Sunday evening, Danny had to leave the party to go to his job as a bartender at a local tavern. Karla dropped him off at work, returning with Jimmy Leibrandt at around 2 a.m. to pick him up. By then, Danny had come up with a plan for gaining revenge on Jerry Lynn Dean. Jerry was a biker and loved nothing more than his Harley. They were going to go around to his place and jack his hog. They'd then dump his pride and joy in a lake or some location where he'd never find it. That would hurt him more than any physical beating ever could. Both Karla and Jimmy Leibrandt loved the idea. And since there was no time like the present, Karla instructed Jimmy to point his car in the direction of Jerry Lynn Dean's apartment.

Jerry's apartment was on the ground floor of a rundown building in a less than salubrious part of town. Turning onto the dimly lit street, Leibrandt immediately switched off the car's headlights and cut the engine, allowing the vehicle to drift to the curb. Then the threesome sat for a while contemplating their next move. Eventually, Garrett instructed Leibrandt to stay in the car while he and Karla went in to case the joint. Moments later, the two of them were scurrying through the dark like spies on a secret mission.

This mission, however, had been ill-planned. They knew that Jerry Lynn kept his Harley parked indoors at night but had not thought about how they were going to get into the apartment without waking him. Neither of them knew how to pick a lock, and breaking a window or forcing the door were, quite obviously, out of the question. As it turned out, they had to do neither. Danny approached the front door, got a tentative grip on the handle, levered it down and pushed. To his surprise, the door swung inward onto the darkened space beyond.

The Harley was exactly where they had expected to find it, standing in the foyer, where it had already marked its territory by leaving a patch of oil on the carpet. But it was at this point that Karla and Danny's half-baked plan hit its first snag. Dean had been working on the motorcycle and it was partially disassembled, parts distributed across the space. An open toolbox was positioned on the floor, greasy tools scattered hither and yon. Against the far wall, as though placed there by fate, stood a pickaxe and a shovel.

The stripped-down motorcycle was a problem, but it was one that was easily overcome. In fact, the revised plan that Danny hastily concocted was even better. In hushed tones, he explained to Karla that they were going to carry away as many motorcycle parts as they could haul, making it impossible for Jerry Lynn to complete his repairs without dipping deep into his pocket. Imagine his anger and frustration when he got up in the morning to find that half of his Harley was missing.

Karla Faye liked the idea. She immediately stooped to begin gathering up some of the motorcycle parts. But she'd barely got started when a light came on in a back room, and she heard the squeak of a mattress as someone got up from a bed. Then footfalls and Jerry Lynn's familiar growl, "Who the hell is out there?"

Karla Faye stood poised, ready to flee. Then Danny took the initiative. He snatched up a hammer from the floor and charged towards the bedroom. Karla Faye followed. She saw Danny swing his weapon and strike Dean on the head, then continue his assault, raining down blow after blow on the fallen man.

Karla would later admit that she was thrilled by the brutal attack. She was also frustrated. She wanted to get in on the act, to exact revenge on behalf of her friend Shawn. As Danny continued bludgeoning Jerry Lynn, she noticed that there was someone else in the bed, a woman cowering on the other side, hiding under the covers. Her murderous rage already roused, Karla Faye ran back to the living room to fetch the pickaxe she'd seen there. Then she returned to the bedroom and joined in the attack.

She lifted the axe and brought it down on the cowering woman, lifted it and brought it down again. The victim, later identified as 32-year-old Deborah Thornton, screamed only once as Karla Faye attacked her chest, her legs, her stomach, and shoulders. Twenty-eight blows were delivered, painting the walls of the small room with Deborah's blood.

But still Karla Faye's bloodlust was not satiated. She now turned her attention towards Jerry Lynn Dean, hacking at his body twenty more times with the axe. Danny then took the weapon from Karla and buried it in Deborah Thornton's heart before the two of them walked away from the blood-drenched crime scene.

It was an incredibly savage double homicide, quite obviously motivated by extreme rage. It was also a crime that was easy to solve. Tucker and Garrett had hardly been discreet about their misdeeds, bragging to anyone who would listen. They also had a less than steadfast accomplice. The police started leaning on informants and were led via the grapevine to Jimmy Leibrandt. He quickly folded under interrogation and would be the state's star witness at the subsequent trial, earning immunity from prosecution in exchange for his testimony.

Karla Faye Tucker and Danny Garrett were indicted for the murders of Jerry Lynn Dean and Deborah Thornton in September 1983. They were tried separately, but the outcome was the same. Both were found guilty, both sentenced to death. Garrett, though, would not keep his date with the executioner. He died of liver disease a short while after his conviction.

That left Karla Faye to take the rap alone, but it would be 14 long years of working through the appeals process before her fate was finally sealed by the US Supreme Court's refusal to intervene. During that time, Karla Faye had become a born-again Christian and had attracted a posse of high-profile backers to her cause. It did her no good. With all other avenues exhausted, a clemency appeal was lodged with Texas governor George W. Bush, who turned her down. Karla Faye Tucker was executed by lethal injection on February 3, 1998.

Karen Lee Huster

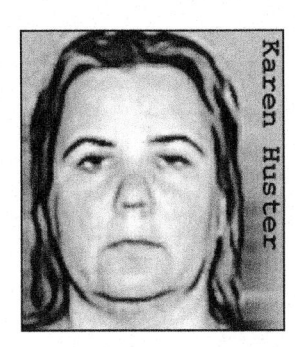

Divorce can be a messy business, and it can be particularly hard on children, those innocent pawns who sometimes find themselves caught in the midst of a fractious separation. This is particularly true when there is a custody battle involved. Then the child might be called on to take sides, might be manipulated or threatened, might be shuttled between one parental home and the other. Many find themselves left with psychological baggage which they carry with them into adulthood. For others, the children of Karen Lee Huster, for example, the cost is even greater.

Karen had married Michael Huster in 1977 and had given him two children during the course of their 19-year union – Johnathon, born 1978, and Elisabeth Ann, who entered the world on September 26, 1986. The marriage, though, was a troubled one, with the couple separating and reconciling several times before an irreparable breakdown in November 1995. Then Mike moved out, taking Johnathon with him and relocating to California. Elisabeth stayed with her mother, although Mike made it clear that he intended filing for full custody during the divorce proceedings. Regrettably he'd never get that chance. On August 31, 1996, 8-year-old Elisabeth Huster attended a wedding with her mother in Cedar Mill, Oregon. She was never seen alive again.

Over the months that followed, Michael Huster made several attempts to see his daughter, only to be rebuffed by his estranged wife. Eventually, in desperation, he contacted Bethany Elementary School, where Elisabeth should have been attending fifth grade classes. To his surprise, the school principal informed him that his daughter had not been enrolled for that academic year. Concerned now, Mike started calling friends and relatives, only to discover that none of them had seen Elisabeth either. It was then that he contacted the police in Portland, Oregon, and reported his daughter missing.

Karen Huster, described by those who knew her as vindictive, bitter, and perpetually angry, was her usual obnoxious self when police officers arrived at her door in December 1996. She told the officers that she had sent Elisabeth to live with relatives in California but refused to give the location. According to her, she had done it for Elisabeth's own protection, since she was afraid that Michael might abduct or even harm the child. In support of this claim, she cited an incident in 1995 when Michael had been arrested for assaulting her during an argument and had subsequently been slapped with a restraining order.

That excuse was enough to hold the authorities at bay…for now. But as the Portland police department continued its missing person investigation, some worrisome details began to emerge. The most troubling of these was the revelation that Karen had held a garage sale in September 1996, just a week after her daughter was last seen alive.

She had used that sale to sell off Elisabeth's toys, clothes, and bedding.

By May 1997, the police had still found no trace of the missing girl, and an arrest warrant was issued for Karen Huster, citing custodial interference. Offered probation if she revealed Elisabeth's whereabouts, Karen flatly refused and was sentenced to two years in prison. She walked free in February 1999 but was soon in trouble again when she was arrested for burglarizing a friend's house and stealing clothing and identity documents. The sentence this time was six months.

But if Karen thought that her troubles regarding her missing child had gone away, she was sorely mistaken. Extensive searches had turned up no trace of Elisabeth, and the authorities had by now begun to suspect that she was dead. Their suspicions were given weight when several of Karen's cellmates came forward and claimed that Karen had admitted killing her daughter and had boasted that the police would never find the body.

In April of 2000, an Oregon grand jury handed down an indictment of first-degree homicide against Karen Huster for the murder of her daughter. Karen, however, had no intention of waiting around for her day in court. She promptly disappeared, fleeing first to Kingman, Arizona, and later showing up in Canoga Park, California, where she moved in with 73-year-old James Cameron at the Parc Place Club Apartments.

In November 2000, the Los Angeles police department received an anonymous tip-off about a possible homicide at Parc Place. Officers responded to the scene and knocked on the door of the unit the tipster had mentioned. Getting no response, they forced the lock and entered. Inside, they found a middle-aged woman with superficial slashes to her arms, apparently as the result of a half-hearted suicide attempt. It was soon apparent why the woman might have wanted to kill herself. On the stove, officers found a crock pot with a human head inside, broiling in curry powder and garlic, the condiments added in a vain attempt to mask the stench of cooking flesh and brain matter. The rest of the body was found dismembered and packed into a freezer. The female occupant of the apartment was immediately placed under arrest.

The murder victim was soon identified as James Cameron. According to neighbors, Cameron was a long-time resident of the building but had only recently begun living with the suspect, who he had told several tenants was his wife. As to the identity of the woman, that was more difficult to establish. She had refused to give her name to detectives and had been booked as a 'Jane Doe.' It was only when the police ran her prints that the learned who she really was – Karen Huster, a fugitive from a murder rap in Oregon.

With her identity uncovered, Huster suddenly had a lot to say about the death of James Cameron. She claimed that Cameron had died of a heart attack inside the apartment. This had put her in a difficult situation since she couldn't report the death without being identified as a wanted felon and returned to Oregon. It had left her with no option but to undertake the unpleasant task of dismembering and concealing the corpse.

Investigators were extremely skeptical of Huster's story. But, to their surprise, the autopsy results backed it up. Cameron had indeed been suffering from heart disease, and there were no apparent signs of foul play on his body. Cause of death was entered as heart failure.

Karen Huster was off the hook for the murder of James Cameron, but she still had to answer for the whereabouts of her daughter. Extradited to Oregon, Huster continued to insist that she had entrusted Elisabeth to relatives in order to protect the child from her father. But by the time the matter came to trial in February 2002, she was singing a different tune. Now she was admitting murder but pleading insanity. According to her latest account, she'd had a vision of angels, beseeching her to entrust Elisabeth to their care. She'd done so on September 1, 1996, shooting the child in the head with a .22 pistol. She had then dismembered the body and disposed of the remains in the Pacific Ocean, dropping them from the side of a boat she'd hired.

It was a far from convincing story, and the prosecution was quick to jump on the inconsistencies. If Karen Huster had killed her daughter in the midst of a psychotic episode, how was it that she'd had the perceptiveness to dispose of the body? How was it that she'd spent years lying about Elisabeth's whereabouts? Karen had a ready, if tenuous, explanation. She said that she had been under severe financial stress at the time, unemployed, and with the bank about to foreclose on her home. She had disposed of the body herself because she had not had money to pay for a funeral.

Picking up on Huster's financial woes, her attorney then produced an expert witness to testify that stress over her finances and failed marriage had produced a brief psychotic disorder which had coincided with the killing of her daughter. She had immediately regretted her action and had decided to kill herself but had lacked the fortitude to go through with it.

To those in the courtroom it must have sounded fanciful and self-serving. A far more likely explanation was the one offered by the prosecution, that Karen Huster, a woman known for her explosive temper and perpetually dark mood, had decided to get back at her estranged husband. She had done so in the way that she knew would scar him more than any other, by taking the life of the little girl that he held so dear. That was the version accepted by the jury as they found Karen Huster guilty of murder and sane at the time that she'd committed the act. She was sentenced to life in prison with a minimum term of 25 years to be served before she becomes eligible for parole.

Mary Ann Cotton

Mary Ann Robson was born in the village of Low Moorsley, County Durham, in October 1832. Her parents were poor folk, her father a miner in nearby East Rainton. Like most lower-class children of her era, Mary Ann had a harsh upbringing, her father's paltry wages barely enough to pay for the family's food and lodgings. Those who knew her spoke of her prettiness as a child and her beauty as a young woman. Perhaps this is true – she was certainly able to snare a succession of husbands and lovers – but the famous photograph of her taken after her arrest, shows a rather plain, middle-aged woman.

Mary Ann's father was a strict Methodist who did not believe in sparing the rod on his children. He also insisted that Mary Ann and her younger brother Robert participate in various church activities. When Mary Ann was eight, the family moved to the nearby village of Murton where she was enrolled at the local school. About a year after this move, Mary Ann's father was killed after falling 150 feet down a mine shaft at the Murton Colliery.

The death of their only breadwinner cast a dark shadow over the Robson family. There was a very real fear that they would be separated and end up on the streets or in the workhouse. However, this fate was averted when Mary Ann's mother Margaret remarried in 1843.

From the very beginning, Mary Ann had trouble getting on with her new stepfather George Stott. He did not like Mary Ann, and the feeling was mutual. Still, she endured until the age of 16, when she left home to work as a servant in a wealthy household in South Hetton. Mary Ann was a hard worker but, by all accounts, also sexually precocious. Not long after her arrival, the village was awash with talk of her trysts with a local clergyman.

Ignoring the gossip, Mary Ann spent three years in service at South Hetton before leaving to complete an apprenticeship as a dressmaker. In 1852, now aged 20, she married colliery laborer William Mowbray by whom she had become pregnant. The couple moved to Plymouth, Devon, where over the next four years Mary Ann gave birth to five children, four of whom died in infancy from gastric fever. Infant mortality rates were high in England at the time, but even by those standards, the Mowbrays appear to have been particularly unlucky parents.

And tragedy followed them on their return to the North East as well. Three more children were born, all of who succumbed to mysterious gastric ailments.

Perhaps because the marriage was so dogged by tragedy, it was not a happy one. The couple argued frequently, usually about Mary Ann's obsession with money. Eventually the constant bickering got to William, and he quit a very good job as a foreman at South Hetton Colliery to become a fireman on the steamer Newburn, out of Sunderland. This frequently took him away from home, leaving Mary Ann to care for the surviving children.

In January 1865, William suffered a workplace accident and returned home to nurse an injured foot. Mary Ann attended him during this time, although he had regular house calls from a doctor. Within weeks, he died suddenly of an intestinal disorder. William's life had been insured by the British and Prudential Insurance Co. Mary Ann profited to the extent of £35, equivalent to about half a year's wages for a manual laborer at the time.

Shortly after her husband's death, Mary Ann moved her remaining children to Seaham Harbour where she struck up a relationship with Joseph Nattrass. Nattrass was engaged to be married at the time, and Mary Ann tried desperately to break up the engagement. Unable to do so, she eventually moved back to Sunderland. But not before burying her three-year-old daughter, leaving her with only one living child out of the nine she had given birth to.

Back in the northeast, Mary Ann found employment at the Sunderland Infirmary, where she became a favorite with staff and patients alike due to her diligence and friendly nature. One patient in particular, an engineer named George Ward, took a liking to Mary Ann. In August 1865, not long after his discharge from the Infirmary, George and Mary Ann were married at a church in Monkwearmouth. Mary Ann's surviving daughter, Isabella, meanwhile had been shipped off to live with her maternal grandmother.

George Ward had been in good health at the time of his discharge from the Infirmary. But soon after he married Mary Ann, he began to complain of chronic stomach problems and paralysis in his limbs. Despite the diligent efforts of his doctors, he died in October 1866. Mary Ann again collected an insurance payout.

A month later she showed up in Pallion and was hired as a housekeeper to shipwright James Robinson. Robinson's wife Hannah had recently died, and part of Mary Ann's remit was to care for the children. Unsurprisingly, death soon visited the Robinson home, the baby of the family dying of a mysterious stomach ailment just before Christmas 1866. James Robinson, still grieving the loss of his wife, was distraught at the death of his child. Fortunately, Mary was there to provide solace – and more. She was soon pregnant with Robinson's child.

In March 1867, just as she and James Robinson were discussing marriage plans, Mary Ann received word that her mother was ill. By the time she returned to her parental home, though, the elderly woman was doing much better. Still, Mary Ann decided to stay awhile, to nurse her mother back to health. Soon after, Margaret Robson began complaining of new symptoms, unrelated to her original illness – she began experiencing severe stomach cramps. Nine days after Mary Ann's arrival, she was dead.

Mary Ann returned to the Robinson household, bringing with her young Isabella (who had been living with her grandmother). Isabella arrived in perfect health but soon developed an incapacitating stomach ailment, as did two of Robinson's children. By the end of April 1867, all three were dead.

With the death of two more of his children, James Robinson must have been wondering what he'd done to deserve so much heartbreak. Nonetheless, he appears not to have suspected any wrongdoing on Mary Ann's part. In early August, he put his mourning aside to wed Mary Ann at St Michael's, Bishopwearmouth. The couple's first child, Mary Isabella, was born in late November. By March 1868, she had succumbed to a mystery illness.

James Robinson, meanwhile, had become suspicious of his wife constantly pestering him to insure his life. Then he learned of debts of over £60 that Mary Ann had run up behind his back. He also found out that a number of household bills had gone unpaid, Mary Ann apparently pocketing the money he'd given her to settle them. The last straw came when his children told him that their stepmother had sent them to pawn various household items. Angered, he threw Mary Ann out. She left taking their young daughter with her. The child would later be returned to James Robinson after Mary Ann abandoned her with an acquaintance.

Mary Ann's worst nightmare had come true – she was penniless and homeless, living on the streets. Then in early 1870, she met a friend, Margaret Cotton, whose brother, Frederick, had been recently widowed. Playing cupid, Margaret introduced the pair. Within months, she was dead of an undetermined stomach ailment, and Mary Ann was left to console the grieving Frederick. That solace, apparently, when way beyond providing a shoulder to cry on. She was soon pregnant with his child.

The couple was married in September 1870 at St Andrew's, Newcastle-upon-Tyne, Mary Ann not bothering to mention the fact that she was still legally married to James Robinson. She set up housekeeping in Cotton's home and secretly insured the lives of Frederick and his two sons Frederick Jr. and Charles.

After giving birth to a son, Robert, in early 1871, Mary Ann learned that her former lover, Joseph Nattrass, was no longer married and was living in the nearby town of West Auckland. After rekindling the romance with Nattrass, she convinced Frederick to move their family there. By year's end, Frederick was dead of gastric fever, and Mary Ann had moved in with Nattrass. She had, of course, also received another insurance payout.

At around this time, Mary Ann was hired as a nurse to John Quick-Manning, an excise officer who was recovering from smallpox. Following a now familiar pattern, she was soon pregnant by her employer. Marriage, however, was out of the question. Joseph Nattrass was still around, and Mary Ann was also encumbered by her infant son and by Frederick Cotton's two children. Not that this was a problem. She soon got to work clearing the decks.

Frederick Cotton Jr. died in March 1872, and baby Robert soon followed. Then Nattrass became ill with gastric fever and died, but not before changing his will and leaving everything he owned to Mary Ann. Now only Charles Cotton stood as an impediment to her plans.

In July 1872, Mary Ann asked a parish official, Thomas Riley, if Charles could be committed to the workhouse. Riley said that it would only be possible if she accompanied him, which she declined. She told Riley that the boy was sickly anyway and predicted that, "I won't be troubled long. He'll go like all the rest of the Cotton family." Riley was surprised by the comment as he'd recently met Charles and found the boy to be in perfectly good health.

Five days later, Riley was shocked to learn that Charles Cotton had died, just as Mary Ann had predicted. Suspecting foul play, he went to the village police office and reported Mary Ann's comments about her stepson's imminent death. He also visited the doctor who had written the death certificate, indicating gastric fever as cause of death. He, too, confessed that he was baffled by the boy's sudden demise.

Mary Ann, meanwhile, was pressing the insurance company to pay out on the policy. On learning that payment was being delayed due to the death certificate, she called on the doctor and was startled to learn that there was to be a formal inquiry. Mary Ann must have feared the worst at this point, but the subsequent inquest seemed to vindicate her, finding that Charles had died of natural causes.

Charles Cotton was duly buried, and Mary Ann collected her insurance payout. But her uncanny run of luck was about to come to an end. A local newspaper picked up on the story and ran a series of articles which hinted that Mary Ann Cotton had been involved in a number of other mysterious deaths. Soon the small town of West Auckland was awash with rumor and suspicion. Even Mary Ann's latest paramour, John Quick-Manning, was affected. He showed her the door.

With the whispering campaign well under way, Mary Ann began making preparations to leave town. She was dissuaded from doing so by friends, who said it would look suspicious.

Unbeknownst to her, moves were already afoot to prove that she was a murderess. A doctor who had participated in the inquest had kept some tissue samples from Charles Cotton's stomach. He now subjected those samples to a new round of testing, checking specifically for the presence of arsenic. Soon he reported his findings to the authorities, stating that he'd found lethal levels of the poison in the boy's stomach lining. Six exhumations were then ordered, including those of Frederick Cotton and Joseph Nattrass. When tests showed that they too had been poisoned, a warrant was issued for Mary Ann.

Mary Ann Cotton's trial began in March 1873, delayed by the birth of her daughter by John Quick-Manning. As was often the practice in those days, she was charged with just one murder, that of her stepson, Charles Cotton.

But one charge was all that was needed. The case against the accused poisoner was damning. There was evidence of her purchases of arsenic, a long list of suspicious deaths in her past, and her statements to Thomas Riley about Charles Cotton's imminent death. Yet, Mary Ann remained steadfast in the face of the evidence. She swore that she had done nothing to harm Charles and insisted that he'd inhaled arsenic fumes from the wallpaper in the Cotton home. Unfortunately for Mary Ann, the jury didn't believe her. It took just 90 minutes to return a guilty verdict. The judge then sentenced Cotton to hang.

Mary Ann Cotton died on the gallows at Durham County Jail on March 24, 1873. According to contemporary accounts, the execution was botched, with the heartless poisoner thrashing around at the end of the rope for over three minutes before she died.

Undoubtedly one of Britain's most prolific serial killers, it is estimated that Cotton was responsible for as many as 22 deaths. These included three of her husbands, eleven children, five stepchildren, her mother, her friend Margaret Cotton, and her lover Joseph Nattrass. Such was her notoriety that she was commemorated in a popular children's rhyme, which endured for over a century;

"Mary Ann Cotton,
She's dead and she's rotten!
She lies in her bed,
With her eyes wide open.
Sing, sing!
Oh, what can I sing?
Mary Ann Cotton is tied up with string.
Where, where?
Up in the air, selling black puddings a penny a pair."

Blanche Taylor Moore

Born in Tarheel, North Carolina, on February 17, 1933, Blanche Kiser grew up in an abusive home. Her father, Parker Kiser, was a lay preacher whose behavior hardly matched his professed love of the holy scriptures. He was a gambler, a heavy drinker, and a womanizer. He also saw no problem in bringing his drinking buddies home to have sex with his pretty teenaged daughter. Blanche was barely into her teens at the time, but she somehow endured the abuse until she was 19. Then she escaped her father's malignant influence by marrying a man named James Taylor.

But if Blanche thought that wedded bliss was the answer to her problems, she was sorely mistaken. Taylor turned out to be a younger version of Parker Kiser, a hard-drinking gambler who made a habit of blowing his family's housekeeping money on poker and horse racing. It meant that Blanche had to go out to work while also raising the couple's two children, Vanessa, born in 1953, and Cindi in 1959.

Not that Blanche minded being a working mom. She enjoyed her job, and she was good at it. Having started as a packer at a Kroger supermarket in Burlington, North Carolina, she soon worked herself up to cashier. By 1960, she'd been promoted to head cashier, a position she'd obtained (according to some colleagues) by sleeping her way through the store's entire management team.

In 1962, a new assistant manager was appointed at the supermarket. Raymond Reid was married and the father of two young children, but that in no way discouraged Blanche from pursuing him. She started flirting with Reid almost from day one and, although he initially showed little interest, she was not discouraged. It would take her three years, but eventually she bedded him. Almost immediately thereafter, she began pestering him to leave his wife.

While all of this was going on, there was some stability at last to Blanche's home life. Her husband, James, had become a born-again Christian and had given up the booze and gambling. And Blanche had finally made peace with her father, a good thing too, as it turned out, because shortly after they were reunited, Parker Kiser became ill. Within weeks, he was dead, his death attributed to a heart attack, even though his symptoms – severe stomach cramps, diarrhea, projectile vomiting, and delirium – were inconsistent with that diagnosis.

Blanche appeared to accept the old man's death with stoic resolve, unsurprising perhaps since the two of them had never been close. Over the years that followed, she continued to secretly date Raymond Reid and kept up the pressure on him to leave his wife.

Did Blanche really believe that he'd do so? Perhaps not, because in 1970, when Reid informed her that he'd walked out on his family, she was caught off guard. While she'd been pressurizing Reid to end his marriage, she'd given little consideration to how she would end her own. The timing of Reid's announcement had also come at a bad time. James's mother, Isla Taylor, had recently fallen ill, and Blanche had been nursing her.

Still, such details had a way of working themselves out in Blanche Taylor's universe. Within weeks of Reid leaving his wife, Isla Taylor was dead, her symptoms remarkably similar to those Blanche's father had suffered. Then, in September 1971, James himself became ill. First, he developed a bad case of the flu, which he just could not shake. Then, he began suffering diarrhea, swollen glands, and hair loss. Painful blisters appeared on his hands and feet, and there was blood in his stool and urine. He died in hospital on October 2, shortly after eating some ice cream that Blanche had brought him.

Following Taylor's death, Blanche and Raymond Reid took their relationship public. But the dynamic had changed. Now it was Raymond making the running and Blanche applying the brakes. He wanted to get married, but she insisted that they take things slow. In truth, she had tired of Reid. With the "forbidden fruit" element of their relationship removed, she found him just a little bit boring. Her sights were already set elsewhere, on the newly appointed Kroger regional manager, Kevin Denton.

Denton proved much easier to land than Raymond Reid, but he also knew what he wanted from Blanche, and it wasn't the serious relationship that she was after. After a few turns at a cheap motel, he told her it was over. Enraged, Blanche filed a sexual harassment suit against Denton and Kroger, forcing Denton to resign and her employer to pay up $275,000 in an out-of-court settlement. Next, Blanche turned her never-ending quest for cash to insurance fraud, netting two payouts due to fires at her home.

In April 1985, there was a new man in Blanche Taylor's life, the Rev. Dwight Moore, pastor of the Carolina United Church of Christ. But there was an obstacle. Raymond Reid was still in the picture, and despite her flirtation with Kevin Denton, he still hoped that Blanche would accept his marriage proposal.

In early 1986, Reid developed a severe case of shingles. By April, he was hospitalized with diarrhea, vomiting, and loss of feeling in his hands and feet. By October he was dead, his body having gained sixty pounds in retained fluids, bloating so severely that it caused his skin to rip. Blanche had been a constant visitor during his hospitalization, bringing him regular food treats from home. She netted $30,000 from Reid's estate, plus more than $45,000 in life insurance.

As always, Blanche showed little reaction to the loss of a man she'd professed to love. Instead, she stepped up her pursuit of Reverend Moore, gleefully accepting his marriage proposal. Their wedding was initially set for August 23, 1987, but was postponed after Blanche was diagnosed with breast cancer and had to undergo a mastectomy. The date was then reset for November 27, 1988, but three weeks before the nuptials, there was another health scare, this time involving Rev. Moore. He developed an inexplicable case of chronic diarrhea and vomiting.

Reverend Moore might have been flummoxed by his sudden turn of ill health, but his bride-to-be could quite easily have enlightened him. She'd been slipping arsenic into his food. Why she'd done so at this point, when there was no real dividend in it, has never been adequately explained. Perhaps Blanche Taylor Moore, like so many serial killers before her, had developed a taste for murder.

Nonetheless, Blanche must have realized that killing her fiancé after the nuptials were completed would be more profitable. Almost as quickly as Rev. Moore's symptoms had appeared, they suddenly vanished. By April 1989, he was well enough to go ahead with the wedding, and on the 21st of that month, he and Blanche tied the knot. They honeymooned in Montclair, New Jersey.

But the reverend's return to health would be short-lived. Back home on April 26, he suddenly collapsed after eating a pastry given to him by his wife. He was rushed to North Carolina Memorial, where a standard toxicology screen turned up the last thing doctors had been expecting. The preacher had been dosed with twenty times the lethal amount of arsenic.

There was only ever one viable suspect, and despite Rev. Moore's protestations that his wife would never harm him, Blanche was taken into custody on June 6, 1989. She denied poisoning her husband, offering instead the improbable explanation that Moore had been depressed and had probably taken the arsenic himself, in a suicide attempt. Then, the police learned that Blanche had been pestering Moore to make her the sole beneficiary of his life insurance policies. That, in turn, led them to another life policy that had dropped into her lap as the result of a suspicious death. Exhumations were then ordered on Raymond Reid, James Taylor, Parker Kiser, and Isla Taylor. All showed evidence of arsenic poisoning.

Blanche Taylor Moore would be tried for only one murder, that of Raymond Reid. Found guilty on that charge, she was sentenced to death. She currently awaits execution at the North Carolina Correctional Institution for Women.

Martha Rendell

The image of the evil stepmother has endured in human consciousness since the Grimm Brothers first published Snow White back in 1812. It gives stepmothers the world over a bad name but, of course, it is mostly a cliché. Most stepmothers are as loving to their acquired offspring as their biological counterparts. Most, but not all. Around the turn of the 20th century, in Perth, Australia, lived an ogress who was the very epitome of the wicked stepmother stereotype. Her name was Martha Rendell, and she's quite possibly the most evil woman in the annals of Australian crime.

Martha Rendell was born August 10, 1871, in Adelaide, South Australia. Little is known about her early life, but we do know that she grew to be a promiscuous teenager, leaving home at 16 and over the next three years delivering three children by different men. Yet, despite offers from her illicit bed partners, she married none of them. Instead, she set her sights on a married man by the name of Thomas Nicholls Morris.

Morris had already fathered nine children by his wife when he and Martha began sleeping together. Their affair, however, did not remain a secret for long. Adelaide, at that time, was no more than a rural backwater, and small town gossip soon began circulating. Eager to escape the scandal, Morris decided it was best to seek a new start elsewhere. In 1900, he told Martha it was over, packed up his family, and left Adelaide for Perth, Western Australia. Martha, however, was not so easily cast aside. She soon followed her lover to the west coast, abandoning her three children in the process.

Arriving in Perth within weeks of the Morris clan, Martha found work as a domestic servant in a well-to-do household. Thomas Morris was perhaps not best pleased to see the lover he'd left behind, but Martha could be persuasive when she needed to be, and she soon won him over with her protestations of undying love. After eliciting promises from her that they'd keep things discreet this time around, he fell back into her arms.

And so it continued over the next six years, with Mrs. Morris none the wiser. Then, in April 1906, Morris suddenly announced to his wife that he was leaving her and setting up home with Martha. And if that were not bad enough for the poor woman, he also took his five youngest children off with him, housing them in the decrepit East Perth shack where he and Martha were living.

Martha had been nagging Thomas for years to leave his wife so, at first, this must have seemed like a victory to her. But the sweet taste of success soon turned bitter as the harsh reality of the situation set in. This wasn't the romantic idyll she'd imagined. Thomas was required to work long hours to support his large family, and it seemed that

Martha saw him less now than when they'd been living apart. Left to care for five children who clearly despised her, she spent her days cooking and cleaning and scrubbing clothes, longing wistfully for her lover's return. When he did arrive, late in the evening, he was usually exhausted and often irritable. This was not what Martha had signed on for. Alone and friendless, living in abject poverty, her resentment took root and flourished. Soon she'd find an outlet for that hatred.

In July 1907, Thomas Morris's second youngest child, Annie, began complaining of a sore throat. A doctor was called, but despite his ministrations, the child's condition continued to worsen. Eventually, her throat was so inflamed that she was unable to eat and found it difficult even to swallow liquids. She died in great pain on July 28, 1907, with the family physician, Dr. James Cuthbert, issuing a certificate that cited cause of death as diphtheria.

Thomas Morris was close to his children, and he took little Annie's death badly. But there was worse to come. On October 6, 1907, five-year-old Olive was dead, apparently from the same disease. And a year later, there was a third death in the Morris household when 14-year-old Arthur succumbed to symptoms that were almost identical to those of his siblings.

In April 1909, six months after Arthur's death, 15-year-old George Morris complained of a sore throat after drinking a cup of tea prepared by his stepmother. Martha then suggested coating his tonsils with her "special medicine," but George refused. He'd already seen what that vile elixir had done to his siblings. In fact, the incident prompted George to decide that he no longer wanted to live under the same roof as his father and stepmother. He ran away, fleeing to his mother's home, just a few blocks away.

Since George was by now of working age, Thomas Morris made very little effort to track him down. Thomas's neighbors, however, noticed the boy's absence and it made them suspicious. They'd already seen three children die at the Morris residence, and they feared that George might be the fourth. One of them, therefore, reported the boy's disappearance to the police.

A detective named Harry Mann was assigned to look into the case. And he was soon hearing horror stories about the abuse suffered by the Morris children at the hands of their stepmother. Neighbors told of screams of agony and terror coming from the house, of young Annie beaten so badly that she was unable to walk, of Martha "rocking back and forth in ecstasy," while one of the little girls lay writhing on the floor at her feet. Then, after the runaway George was located, he added another level of detail. His stepmother had poisoned Annie, Olive, and Arthur by coating their throats with her "special medicine," he said. And she'd been trying to poison him, too, which was why he'd run away.

The evidence thus far amounted to little more than hearsay and unfounded allegation. But Inspector Mann deemed it sufficient to charge Martha Rendell with murder and Thomas Morris as an accomplice. Both vociferously proclaimed their innocence, but autopsies on the exhumed bodies would prove Rendell a liar, as well as a sadist of breathtaking depravity. Hydrochloric acid was found in the throat tissue of each child. It appeared that Martha Rendell had coated the back of the children's throats with the corrosive substance, something that would have left them in agony. Death, however, would have come as a side effect of this sadistic practice. The acid would have caused severe inflammation, resulting in the narrowing of the throat passage and making it impossible for the children to swallow. The Morris children had died of starvation.

Martha Rendell went on trial in August 1909, charged with three counts of murder. Thomas Morris had by now been acquitted of all charges, but there would be no such latitude for the evil stepmother. She was eventually convicted of one murder, that of Arthur Morris, and sentenced to hang. That sentence was carried out on October 6, 1909, coincidentally the first anniversary of Arthur's death and the second anniversary of Olive's passing.

FOOTNOTE: Martha Rendell was the last woman to be executed in Western Australia. She shares a grave at Fremantle Cemetery with Eric Edgar Cooke, Perth's notorious "Night Caller" who went to the gallows fifty years after her.

Michelle Knotek

James "Mac" McClintock was a WWII veteran who had survived the attack on Pearl Harbor. He was a tough old bird who lived in a house that he owned on Monohon Landing Road in South Bend, Washington, sharing the residence with his beloved black Labrador, Sissy. He maintained some independence by using a motorized wheelchair to traverse the sidewalks of the town's main drag. But the years had been tough on James. Recently, he'd suffered a number of strokes, and he was also afflicted with heart problems. At 81, he was no longer able to care for himself. In September 2001, he decided to hire a full time caregiver. The person he chose for the task was 46-year-old Michelle Knotek.

On the face of it, Michelle was well-qualified for the job. Between 2000 and 2001, she had been employed by the Olympic Area Agency on Aging, and it was there that she'd first encountered James McClintock and struck up a rapport with him. But the agency had terminated Knotek's services in April 2014, and she was at a loose end. The live-in caregiver arrangement seemed a good fit for both parties.

And, at first, it appeared to work well. In fact, McClintock was so impressed by Michelle's work that he soon wrote out a will in her favor, leaving her his $140,000 home and around $8,800 in cash. He also entrusted the care of his much-loved dog to her, the only stipulation being that Sissy was to be buried beside him once she passed on. McClintock was certain that he would go before the dog, and he was right. Six months after making out the will in Knotek's favor, the police were called to his home where they found McClintock dead, with an ugly welt on his head. Michelle claimed that he had fallen out of his wheelchair, and her story was believed. Many of South Bend's 3,000 residents had seen Mac fall out of his chair over the years and had helped him back into it. His death certificate recorded cause of death as "undetermined."

In October of 2001, a month after James McClintock's death, Michelle Knotek had another disabled man in her care. Ron Woodworth was a local eccentric with a record for various misdemeanors, including check fraud and harassment. The 56-year-old Vietnam vet was college-educated with a degree from Berkeley. But his behavior had grown increasingly bizarre over the years as both his mental health and personal hygiene faltered. This led inevitably to a loss of employment and to him being evicted from the trailer he'd been renting. Thereafter, there were at least four anti-harassment petitions, one of them filed by his own mother. No one considered Woodworth to be particularly dangerous, but most gave him a wide berth. Most, that is, except Michelle Knoteck. She befriended Woodworth in late 2001 and, shortly thereafter, invited him to live at the home that she had inherited from James McClintock.

But this apparent act of altruism wasn't all that it seemed. Over the next two years, neighbors would often see and hear Ron Woodworth being physically and mentally abused by Michelle Knotek and her husband, Dave. Often, they'd see him doing chores in the yard during the frigid winter months wearing nothing but his underwear. On one occasion, he was forced to jump barefoot from a second-floor window onto the gravel path below, suffering fractures and severe lacerations as a result. Neighbors would hear Michelle shouting at him, and sometimes they'd hear Woodworth screaming in pain. It would later emerge that Michelle enjoyed pouring boiling water or acid over his feet as a form of "punishment." And then, in July 2003, Ron Woodworth was suddenly gone.

Woodworth's disappearance might well have gone unreported but for a call to Pacific County police in August of 2003. The call was from one of Michelle Knotek's adult daughters who told the police about the abuse that Woodworth had suffered at her mother's hands. That report brought officers to the Monohon Landing Road residence, and it was during a search of the property that they uncovered a freshly dug grave containing the remains of Ron Woodworth. Michelle and David Knotek were then placed under arrest.

That, however, was far from the end of the matter. Once in custody, David Knotek quickly cracked and admitted that he and his wife had been involved in two other murders, both of which had occurred in 1994.

The first of the 1994 victims was a 36-year-old hairdresser named Kathy Loreno. Kathy had become friends with Michelle Knotek in 1991, probably after Michelle started having her hair done at the salon where Kathy worked as a stylist. At the time, Kathy was living at home with her mother, but the relationship deteriorated when she started dating a man her mother didn't like. When she spoke to Michelle about these problems, Michelle was quick to offer a solution. Kathy could move in with her and Dave and their two teenage daughters. Michelle's nephew, 19-year-old Shane Watson, was also living in the house at the time and Michelle was pregnant with her third child. But there was room enough for all. Kathy happily agreed to the arrangement. Soon after, she would discover a different side to her friend Michelle.

According to testimony later provided by the Knoteks' daughters, Kathy Loreno was beaten, choked, and dragged across the ground by her hair; she was forced to swallow toxic substances, prescription medicines, and large quantities of salt; she had to submit to bizarre "treatments," such as having bleach and salt rubbed into her open wounds. In an echo of the Ron Woodworth case, she was forced to work outside in freezing temperatures, then immersed in a bath of cold water once she was allowed back indoors. She was also starved, causing her to lose over 100 pounds and resulting in her hair and teeth falling out. Towards the end of her life, she was reduced to a skeletal wreck of a human being who could neither walk nor talk. According to David, she had died after choking on her own vomit. (His daughter would dispute this, saying that Michelle had clubbed Kathy to death with a clothes iron.) Thereafter, David and Shane burned the corpse and dumped the ashes in the Pacific Ocean. Bizarrely, David now claimed that he'd only destroyed the body because he was afraid that the police would notice Kathy's "injuries."

Kathy Loreno's family questioned the Knoteks about her whereabouts, of course, but Michelle had a ready-made cover story. She said that Kathy had run away with a truck driver and was now living in Hawaii.

She even produced letters, supposedly written by Kathy, to back up her story. Then, after Kathy's relatives reported her missing, Michelle told the same story to the police, claiming that she and Kathy were still in regular contact and that Kathy wanted nothing to do with her family. Unable to prove otherwise, the police let the matter drop.

Kathy's family, however, was not so easily put off. They hired a private investigator who quickly concluded that Kathy was probably dead and that Michelle and David Knotek had most likely killed her. Unfortunately, he could offer no specific proof to back up his conclusions.

The second person to die inside the Knotek residence that year was Shane Watson. Shane had come to live with the Knoteks in 1992 after moving out of his grandparents' home, where he'd grown up. He was described by them as a pleasant, easygoing boy.

But living in the Knotek household appears to have changed Shane Watson. There is no evidence to suggest that he participated directly in the abuse of Kathy Loreno, but he did nothing to stop it either. In fact, Watson recorded much of the maltreatment on his camcorder, and it was that which decided his fate. He simply knew too much.

In the summer of 1994, Michelle Knotek ordered her husband to take care of the problem. He did that by luring Watson into the garden shed and shooting him in the back of the head with a .22 caliber rifle. Watson's remains were disposed of in the usual way, by burning and dispersal of the ashes. When his grandparents later enquired about him, Kathy told them that he'd moved to Alaska to work on a fishing boat. Now, at last, the truth about his disappearance was known.

David Knotek was charged with the first-degree murder of Shane Watson and with rendering criminal assistance and unlawful disposal of human remains. Michelle was charged with the murders of Kathy Loreno and Ronald Woodworth. Both were looking at long prison terms if found guilty. However, this was a complex case, with prosecutors particularly worried about the absence of evidence that would confirm cause of death. Concerned that a jury might see this as sufficient grounds for an acquittal, they decided to offer the couple a deal, allowing them to plead to lesser charges.

Michelle Knotek entered an Alford plea to one count of second-degree murder and one count of manslaughter. This is a unique legal maneuver whereby the defendant does not admit liability but concedes that the prosecution has sufficient evidence to secure a conviction. Effectively, it is a plea of "no contest."

Prosecutors had agreed on a term of 17 years in exchange for this plea, but Michelle was in for a nasty surprise at trial. The judge deemed the sentence too lenient and added an additional five years, sending her to prison for 22 years. It was still an extremely lenient sentence, given the gravity of her crimes. She is currently serving her time at the Washington Corrections Center for Women in Gig Harbor.

At his trial, David Knotek entered a guilty plea to the second-degree murder of Shane Watson and was sentenced to 15 years in prison. He is currently incarcerated at the Monroe Correctional Complex and is eligible for parole in 2019.

The perpetrators were behind bars, the most sensational case in Pacific County's history resolved to the satisfaction of most parties. But still the questions lingered. What could possibly have motivated a small-town housewife to commit such atrocities? David Knotek's motivation was evident. He was quite obviously the hen-pecked husband of a dominant woman. But what had been Michelle's motive for inflicting such abuse on Kathy Loreno and Ronald Woodworth?

The answers are far from simple. Nothing in Michelle's background hints at the psychopathic monster that she would become. Some who knew her said that she had anger issues and could be volatile and temperamental. Yet she could also be charming and appeared to have a genuine compassion for the vulnerable and downtrodden. Perhaps that was part of her M.O. Like all psychopaths, she was a predator, separating the weak and unwary from the herd. Those who fell for her superficial charm had no idea of the horrible fate that awaited them.

Michelle Knotek has never been charged with the death of James "Mac" McClintock or with any other suspicious deaths that might have occurred in the decade between known murders. Those who have knowledge of this type of killer suggest that there are more than likely other victims.

Terri Rachals

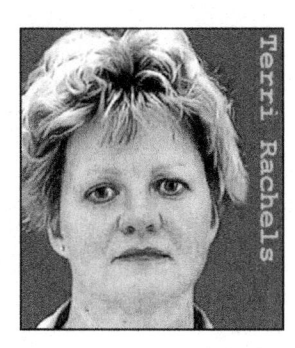

During October and November of 1985, administrators at Phoebe Putney Hospital in Albany, Georgia, noticed an alarming increase in the number of patients who had suffered cardiac arrests while receiving treatment in the hospital's intensive care unit. Six of these patients had died, and the number of casualties would have been higher but for the intervention of medical staff. The deceased had all been seriously ill, but hospital management were still concerned enough to call in the Georgia Department of Human Resources. Their fear was that they might have a serial killer on the wards.

The job of evaluating the sudden spike in the mortality rate at Phoebe Putney fell to Dr. Adelle Franks, an epidemiologist on secondment from the U. S. Center for Disease Control. And she soon uncovered some startling evidence. Examining the number of heart attack deaths at the hospital over the prior year, Dr. Franks found that there had been three months where not a single death had occurred. The highest number of deaths-per-month during the review period was four. This had happened on two occasions.

Yet, during November 1985, 11 patients had suffered heart attacks and five of those had died. It was also telling that all of the deaths had occurred on the 3:00 p.m. to 11:00 p.m. shift. According to Dr. Franks, the probability of this happening by chance "was less than one in a trillion." Her conclusion was that someone had deliberately caused the heart attacks. This was now a matter for the police.

The investigation now passed to the Georgia Bureau of Investigation (GBI) which ordered postmortems on six potential homicide victims. The first of these was 68-year-old Milton Lucas, who had died of an apparent heart attack on October 19, 1985. Then there was Minnie Houck, age 58, who had gone into cardiac arrest and died on November 7. Just three days later, 36-year-old Joe Irwin suffered a similar fate. He was followed to the grave by Roger Parker, also 36, who perished on November 15 despite the best efforts of doctors to save him. Medical staff were also unable to save the life of 73-year-old Andrew Daniels who died on November 24. And finally, there was the most tragic death of all. Norris Morgan was just three years old when he died on November 26.

In addition to these six fatalities, there were at least four cases in which patients had narrowly survived a brush with death. Sam Bentley, George Whiting, Frances Freeman, and Jack Stephens had all suffered unexplained heart attacks in the ICU and were only alive due to the intervention of emergency medics. And there were other deaths, too, which fell outside the review timeframe but nonetheless looked suspicious. The most startling of these was the unexplained demise of 26-year-old Lee Creech, a prison inmate who had been brought to Phoebe Putney for medical treatment but had died on December 21. Cause of death was given as cardiac arrest, but that raised a plethora of questions. How could an apparently healthy 26-year-old, with no history of heart disease, suddenly die of a heart attack? Had someone done something to cause his death? If so, who?

The answer lay in Dr. Franks's report. Franks had listed the primary nurse on duty at the time of eleven cardiac arrests during the month of November. One name stood out. Terri Eden Rachals had been on duty on eight occasions while none of the other 24 nurses working the shift were present more than once. This meant that a heart attack was 26.6 times more likely to occur while Nurse Rachals was on duty. The odds of that being a coincidence were less than zero.

Looking into Rachals background, investigators found that she was a 24-year-old, married mother of one. A native of Hopeful, Georgia, she had been adopted at age two after her mother suffered a nervous breakdown. Her adoptive mother had died of a stroke when Terri was 11, and she'd thereafter been looked after by her adoptive father. She would later claim that he'd sexually assaulted her between the ages of 11 and 16. Whether that is true or not, Terri did well at school and later qualified as a nurse. Her supervisors considered her to be good at her job, although she did show some worrying traits. She was frequently depressed and sometimes spoke of suicide.

Rachals was brought in for questioning and soon cracked under interrogation, admitting that she'd killed at least five patients by injecting lethal doses of potassium chloride into their intravenous drips. She would then watch the EEG and wait until the patient was beyond saving before raising the alarm. Rachals claimed that she'd acted out of mercy and that her elderly victims had begged her to help them die. But that did not make her less of a murderer. It also did not explain why she'd killed two middle-aged men. And it could never justify the killing of three-year-old Norris Morgan.

Terri Rachals was indicted on six counts of murder and twenty counts of aggravated assault. But by the time the matter came to trial in September 1985, Rachels had apparently had a change of heart. She now claimed that her confession had been coerced, and although she did not deny the charges outright, she claimed that she had no memory of tampering with the patients' IV lines. The defense then produced an expert witness who testified that Rachals's struggles with chronic depression caused her to sometimes exist in a fugue state. During these "fugues," she had no conscious control over her actions and acted on "auto-pilot." She may well have spiked her victims' IV units, but she had no recollection of doing so. She should, therefore, be acquitted of murder.

Tenuous as this defense might have seemed to most observers, it was a difficult one to disprove beyond a reasonable doubt. The jury, certainly, appeared to be willing to accept it. They acquitted Rachals on all of the murder charges and all but one of the aggravated assault charges against her. Even on that charge, they found her "guilty but mentally ill."

Terri Rachals was sentenced to a 17-year prison term, plus three years of probation on release. She walked free on April 1, 2003, having served her full term.

Amelia Sach & Annie Walters

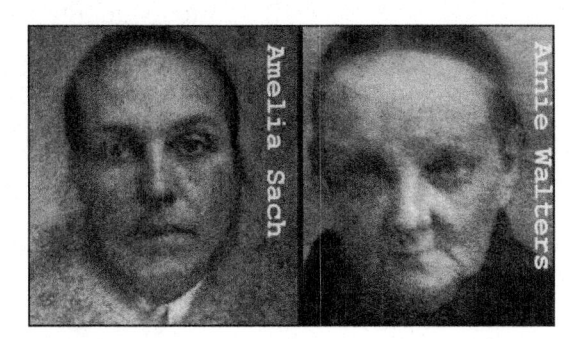

Baby farming... the very name conjures up visions of some malevolent Victorian matron hovering over an unfortunate infant by gaslight, choking or poisoning the poor child, confining its tiny corpse to the depths of some cold canal, and then trundling off to enjoy her ill-gotten gains. Yet not all baby farmers were of this ilk. The vast majority, in fact, provided a valuable service at a time when children born out of wedlock would not even be taken in by an orphanage.

The practice of baby farming operated on a simple principle. A woman engaged in the trade would advertise in the newspaper, offering to care for unwanted babies. This of course was not done out of the goodness of the prospective caregiver's heart. It was a commercial enterprise. For a fee, which was either a weekly stipend or a once-off lump sum, the baby farmer offered to raise the child herself or to find a suitable adoptive home for it. All the mother had to do was drop off the baby, pay the money, and then walk away secure in the knowledge that her child would be cared for.

And if that were the whole story behind baby farming, then it would never have acquired its nefarious reputation. But unfortunately, the industry was unregulated, creating the opportunity for unscrupulous operators to step in, women like Amelia Dyer, who reportedly adopted dozens of children, then strangled them, dumped their bodies in the Thames, and pocketed the adoption fee. Dyer was one of seven baby farmers to be executed for murder between 1871 and 1908. Two more who kept a date with the hangman were Amelia Sach and Annie Walters.

Amelia Sach was born Frances Amelia Thorne in Hampreston, Dorset, on May 5, 1867, the fourth child of ten. Little is known about her childhood, but we do know that she relocated to London in the latter part of the 1890s when her father found work there. After his death, Amelia married a builder named Jeffrey Sach, by whom she later had a daughter named Lillian. The couple set up home in a handsome red-brick terrace in Finchley, North London. There Amelia began operating a "lying-in home," a place where unwed women could stay before giving birth.

The majority of Amelia Sach's clients were poor servant girls who could not afford to take time off work to care for a baby and, in any case, would quickly find themselves out of employment if it were discovered that they had an illegitimate child. It is probably while listening to the tribulations of these unfortunate women that Sach first decided to expand her operation into baby farming. The trade, after all, paid handsomely, up to £50 for arranging an adoption, certainly more than Sach was earning from her nursing home.

We don't know for certain when Amelia Sach switched from post-natal nurse to baby farmer, but we do know that from the early months of 1902, she began making subtle changes to her newspaper advertisements, adding the phrase "Baby can remain." This is key, since it was a euphemism commonly used by baby farmers to indicate that they were prepared to take a child off a desperate mother's hands. Sach was soon inundated with callers.

The proposal that Sach had to offer was undoubtedly attractive. For a fee of just £25, half the going rate, she undertook to find a loving adoptive home for the child. She'd assure the mother that she had a backlist of "well-to-do" clients who were unable to conceive and thus desperate for a child. The darling little thing would be pampered and cossetted, raised in luxury and educated at the finest institutions. It would want for nothing. To a poor uneducated servant girl, the offer was compelling and was seldom refused. It was also wide of the mark.

Amelia Sach made no effort at all to have the infants adopted. Instead she handed them over to her accomplice, Annie Walters, to dispose of. Walters, 54, was a feeble-minded and drug-addicted individual who had once worked as a midwife. Her method of disposal was usually to feed the infant a lethal dose of chlorodyne, a concoction of chloroform, cannabis and opium that was freely available at the time and was sold as a cure for cholera. She'd then wrap the tiny corpse in brown paper and dump it at a railway station or in a back alley. As many as 30 infants may have met their end this way. In at least one case, an innocent woman was executed for murdering her child when the perpetrators were, in fact, Sach and Walters.

Amelia Sach however, should have been more prudent in her choice of partner. Walters, as we have already noted, was somewhat dim-witted and had a liking for both opiates and gin. In her cups, she was prone to making ill-advised comments about her vocation. Most ignored these proclamations as the ramblings of an imbecile, a good thing, too, because many of Walters's assertions could have landed her in deep trouble.

In the winter of 1902, Walters moved to new lodgings at an Islington residence owned by a police officer named Seal. Officer Seal's wife served as the landlady of the premises, and to her, Walters explained that she was employed by an agency that arranged adoptions for unwanted children. This might require her to occasionally have a baby over to spend the night. She wanted to be sure that the arrangement was acceptable. Mrs. Seal assured her that it would be, although she asked Walters to clear it with her on a case-by-case basis.

On November 12, Walters received a telegram from Sach with the cryptic message "Five o'clock tonight. Sach, Finchley." Walters then obtained permission from Mrs. Seal to keep a baby in her room overnight and departed, returning later that evening with a little boy. The following day the child was gone, adopted by a widowed lady in Piccadilly, according to Walters.

On November 15 another telegram arrived, and Walters again got permission to bring the baby home. "This one is going to a coast guard's wife at South Kensington," she told her landlady.

Walters's behavior, though, had begun to cause suspicion in the household. As always, she made a habit of talking too much when she'd been drinking and often made contradictory statements. On one occasion, she brought a baby home which she assured everyone was a girl. However, when Mrs. Seal later changed the baby's diaper (after Walters had passed out), she discovered that the child was actually a boy. Her suspicions roused, Mrs. Seal spoke to her husband. He, in turn, arranged for Annie Walters to be followed.

On November 18, Walters was observed leaving her residence with a tiny bundle in her arms. A plainclothes police officer followed, tracking her all the way to Kensington Station where Walters entered a ladies' restroom and didn't re-emerge. After waiting a while, the officer went to investigate and found Walters holding a dead baby.

The child was the four-day-old son of Ada Galley, a servant girl who had recently given birth at Claymore House. His tiny corpse carried the clear signs of asphyxia, fists clenched, tongue blackened, and swollen lips tinged purple.

Walters admitted to giving the child chlorodyne but claimed it had only been a couple of drops to still the baby's crying. She insisted that she hadn't intended to kill the child. The police officer, however, wasn't buying that explanation. He placed Walters under arrest and charged her with murder.

Annie Walters was taken to South Kensington police station where she quickly talked herself into a corner and, at the same time, implicated Amelia Sach. When officers arrived to take Sach into custody, she denied any knowledge of the crime and even said that she did not know anyone named Annie Walters. Unfortunately for Sach, the telegrams she'd sent to Walters instructing her to pick up children for disposal told a different story. She promptly found herself locked up beside her co-accused.

Sach and Walters were brought to trial at the Old Bailey in January of 1903. There the Crown produced several witnesses, including Lucy Pardoe, a young woman whose child Annie Walters had been summoned to collect on November 12. Miss Pardoe said that she'd paid Amelia Sach £30 and had been assured that her baby was going to a good home.

Another witness spoke of seeing Walters carrying a bundle wrapped in blankets. When the blanket fell away, the witness saw that it was a baby which appeared not to be breathing. When the witness challenged Walters about this, Walters said that the little boy had just undergone an operation and was suffering the effects of chloroform. Before the witness could take the matter further, Walters fled the scene.

As more and more witnesses were called to the stand – Mrs. Seal, her son Albert, and the police constable who had arrested Walters – the evidence against the deadly pair continued to stack up. Yet Sach and Walters still professed their innocence. Even when the all-male jury returned a verdict of guilty against them and the judge sentenced them to death, they continued to claim that they'd done nothing wrong. Those denials would do them no good.

Amelia Sach and Annie Walters were executed side-by-side at Holloway Prison on February 3, 1903. The executioner, H.A. Pierrepoint, later recorded in his memoirs that they did not go to their deaths with dignity. "These two women were baby farmers of the worst kind," he wrote. "They had literally to be carried to the scaffold and protested to the end against their sentences."

The publicity created by the Sach and Walters case went a long way towards eradicating baby farming, although they would not be the last women to be executed for the practice. That dubious record belongs to Rhoda Willis, who was hanged in Wales in 1907. The Children and Young Persons Act, passed in 1908, effectively put an end to the baby farming industry.

Katherine Knight

Katherine Mary Knight was born in Tenterfield, New South Wales, on October 24, 1955. She was the younger of twins, exiting the womb half an hour after her sister, Joy. Her mother, Barbara, already had four boys, Patrick, Martin, Neville, and Barry, from a previous marriage. Another son, Charlie, was conceived with Katherine's father Ken, and the couple would have one more child, Shane, in 1961.

Ken Knight was a slaughterer who worked at abattoirs throughout Queensland and New South Wales before eventually settling in Aberdeen in 1969. It is not the sort of trade that a young girl might aspire to, but from an early age, it was all that Katherine wanted to do. She fulfilled her ambition at 16 when she joined her father at the Aberdeen slaughterhouse. There, she quickly gained a reputation for her tough, uncompromising manner. If anyone offended her, she'd challenge them to a knife fight. No one ever took her up.

Katherine's first job was cutting up carcasses, yet she was often to be found watching the animals actually being killed. Her workmates put it down to an interest in the job. Given what we now know, it was almost certainly more than that.

In 1973, the 17-year-old Katherine fell in love with a truck driver named David Kellett. She moved in with him in October of that year, and they married a year later. Shortly after the wedding, a rumor started doing the rounds in Aberdeen. It appeared that Katherine had attempted to strangle her husband on their wedding night, after his sexual performance failed to live up to her expectations.

Given that unpromising start to married life, it is perhaps unsurprising that the Kellets had a somewhat turbulent union. Katherine was jealous and possessive and dominated her husband physically. Eventually, David could take no more. After the birth of their daughter, Melissa Ann, in May 1976, he abandoned his wife and eloped with another woman.

Katherine was distraught at being cast aside. But true to form, she was also deeply resentful and lusting for revenge. Without David there to direct her rage at, she instead targeted her infant daughter. The day after David's departure, she was seen pushing a baby stroller down the town's main street, swinging it violently from side to side. Later that day, a man found the buggy on nearby railway tracks with two-month-old Melissa still inside. He moved it just in time to save the baby from being obliterated by an oncoming train.

But still, Katherine's ire wasn't sated. Later that same day, she picked up an axe from a woodpile and walked through the streets of the town, swinging the weapon wildly at anyone she encountered. She was arrested and taken to St Elmo's Hospital in Tamworth where postnatal depression was diagnosed. She was released soon after.

Just days later, Katherine accosted a woman that she knew and demanded that the woman drive her to find David. When the woman hesitated, Katherine drew a knife and slashed her across the face. Bleeding profusely, the woman escaped after pulling into a gas station on the pretense of filling her car. Katherine then took a young boy hostage, holding a knife to the child's throat and threatening to behead him. It took several police officers to subdue her, holding her at bay with broomsticks while she slashed wildly at them. This time, she was taken to Morisset Psychiatric Hospital.

But the authorities could not hold her at Morisset indefinitely. Given that she would inevitably be released, the police thought it prudent to track down her estranged husband and warn him. David Kellet's response to the news surprised them. He immediately broke off his new relationship and drove back to Aberdeen to be with his wife, bringing his mother with him for support.

On August 9, 1976, Katherine was released from the psychiatric ward into the custody of her mother-in-law. A couple of days later, she and David picked up Melissa from her maternal grandparents and the family was reunited, moving to a rented bungalow in Woodridge.

But marital bliss was predictably short-lived. It wasn't long before Katherine was abusing her husband again, attacking him with her fists, with metal skillets and, on one occasion, with a hot clothes iron. These frequent fights would be interspersed with rare moments of tenderness between the combatants. In mid-1979, Katherine announced that she was pregnant, and on March 6, 1980, she gave birth to another daughter, Natasha Maree.

David Kellet would endure his wife's violent abuse for four more years. Then, one day in 1984, he came home from work to find Katherine and their two daughters gone. Katherine had returned to her parents' farm just outside of Aberdeen, where she started working again at the local abattoir. She would remain there for another year until a back injury rendered her unable to work, and she was given a disability pension and a State-sponsored house in Aberdeen.

The next unfortunate man to enter Katherine Knight's life was Dave Saunders, a 38-year-old miner from the nearby town of Scone. The couple started dating in 1986 and, at first, the relationship went well. But it wasn't long before Katherine's obsessive jealousy bubbled to the surface. Saunders still maintained an apartment in Scone, and Katherine began accusing him of seeing other women there. Soon the pattern of her violent marriage began repeating itself. She attacked Saunders with anything that was close at hand. Once, she cut the throat of his two-month-old puppy; another time she battered him unconscious with a frying pan; on many occasions, she threw him out of her house. But no sooner had he left than she was on the phone to him, begging him to return.

In June 1987, Katherine gave birth to her third child, another daughter, who she named Sarah. The baby seemed to calm her down. She and Saunders starting talking about marriage and, in 1989, he put down a deposit on a property in Aberdeen. When Katherine's worker's compensation check came through, she paid off the house in full. Then she began decorating it in bizarre fashion.

Every inch of wall space was covered with cow hides, buffalo horns, cow and sheep skulls and deer antlers. In addition, there were animal traps, a huge wooden fork and spoon, a rusted pitchfork and various motorcycle jackets. A scythe hung from the ceiling over the couch. It was the home of Katherine Knight's dreams.

Unfortunately, Katherine's brief encounter with domesticity would not last. During another of her jealous rages, she battered Dave Saunders with a clothes iron, stabbed him with a pair of scissors, and then cut all of his clothes to shreds. Saunders then wisely decided to disappear, quitting his job and leaving the area. Months later, he returned to see his daughter, no doubt thinking that the passage of time would have calmed Katherine down. He was wrong. She attacked him, delivering a brutal beating. Then, to add insult to injury, she filed assault charges, claiming that he had been the aggressor and that she'd been forced to defend herself.

Katherine Knight was clearly not the kind of woman you'd want to tangle with. And she was certainly no beauty. Yet, despite her fearsome reputation, there were still men who were prepared to take up the challenge. The next to step into the breach was John Chillingworth, a former colleague of hers at the Aberdeen slaughterhouse. Their relationship would endure for three years, during which Katherine gave birth to a son, Eric. Chillingworth appears to have been somewhat more resilient than his predecessors. He took his beatings and remained devoted to Katherine. He was genuinely heart-broken when she dumped him for a man named John Price in 1994. Later, he'd have reason to thank his lucky stars.

John Price ("Pricey" to all who knew him) was by all accounts a nice guy. He'd been married before and had three kids, the younger of whom lived with his former wife. The older two children, a teenaged son and daughter, lived with Pricey in a comfortable three-bedroom bungalow on St. Andrews Street in Aberdeen.

Like Katherine's former beaus, Price would have been well aware of her reputation. But the Katherine he grew to know was a different woman to the one depicted in those horror stories. She was loving and devoted, a charming companion and an excellent homemaker who kept his house spotless. He would arrive home each day to find a delicious meal waiting for him. And if he lingered too long at the pub and had too much to drink, a phone call would soon have Katherine driving over to pick him up. Then, there'd be no complaints. She was just glad he'd called her rather than driving home in an inebriated state.

But, of course, this subservient hausfrau version of Katherine was never going to last. It wasn't long before she began slinging accusations of infidelity. Then the fights started, often conducted in public with the lovers going toe-to-toe outside one of their homes or in the street outside a pub where Pricey had been drinking. Price, to his credit, stood his ground, refusing to be subjugated. On several occasions, he broke things off with Katherine, only to be talked around by her promises to reform her ways.

In late 1995, during one of the calmer periods of their relationship, Pricey asked Katherine to move in with him. Perhaps he thought that having Katherine under his roof would reassure her that he was true to her and that her jealous rages were misplaced. Instead, the cohabitation arrangement only seemed escalate the trouble between them. In 1998, after another bitter feud, Katherine videotaped some medical kits Pricey kept in his home. She then sent the tape to his boss, claiming he'd stolen the items from the workplace.

The items had, in fact, been salvaged from a scrapheap where they'd been dumped after passing their expiry date. Still, Pricey was fired. In revenge, he kicked Katherine out of his home, only to take her back again a few months later. Soon they'd fallen back into the old routine of break-up and make-up. Only now, the fights were more frequent and more violent. On February 29, 2000, Pricey showed up at the local hospital with a serious knife wound to his chest. He refused to say who had stabbed him and declined to press charges. However, he did attend the Scone Magistrate's Court the following day. He left the building with a restraining order against Katherine Knight.

But a mere piece of paper wasn't going to discourage an obsessive woman like Katherine. That night, while Pricey was visiting his neighbor, she sneaked into his house and had a shower, then slipped into a sexy, black negligee. When Pricey returned home at around eleven o'clock, he found her waiting in his bed and the two of them had sex. He never had been able to resist her.

The following morning, Wednesday, March 1, a neighbor noticed John Price's truck still standing in the driveway. This was unusual, since Pricey normally left for work early, before 6 a.m. When the truck was still there an hour later, the neighbor became concerned. He went to check on Price, but knocking on a side window drew no response. The neighbor then went to the front of the house. It was then that he noticed blood on the door frame.

The police were called and arrived at around 8 o'clock. Getting no reply when they knocked, they forced a back door and entered the house. They were immediately stopped in their tracks by a gruesome sight. Hanging from a hook in the kitchen was what looked like a complete human skin. Further in, on the lounge floor, lay the decapitated corpse of John Price, entirely flayed. There was blood pooled on the floor and smeared on the walls. Bracing themselves for further horrors, the officers kept searching. The gentle sound of snoring drew them towards the main bedroom, and it was there that they found Katherine Knight, fast asleep on the bed. She'd apparently taken an overdose of sleeping pills.

While an ambulance conveyed Katherine to the hospital, the search of the house continued. And as horrific as the discoveries had been thus far, the worst was yet to come. On the kitchen stove stood a large pot. One of the officers lifted the lid and then quickly dropped it and stepped back. The pot contained John Price's head, stewing with various vegetables. Two prepared meals also sat on the table, each containing two pieces of broiled meat, baked potato, baked pumpkin, zucchini, cabbage, yellow squash and gravy. Beside each plate was a slip of paper with a name written on it, "Becky" and "Jonathan." A third meal had also been prepared but had been thrown out onto the lawn. The flesh would later prove to have been sliced from John Price's buttocks.

From the horrendous evidence at the scene and the subsequent autopsy, a picture emerged of what had happened. After having sex with Price, Katherine Knight had produced a knife and stabbed her lover, delivering 37 deep wounds to his chest and back. She'd then dragged his body into the passage and skinned it, leaving the skin hanging from a hook in the architrave between lounge and kitchen. Then she'd decapitated him and sliced flesh from his buttocks. These had gone into various pots as she prepared three meals, one for herself and one each for Price's son and daughter. Fortunately, the children were away and did not return to be fed their father's butchered flesh. It was also uncertain whether Katherine had eaten any of the macabre meal. Her portion had been thrown out into the garden.

That was the police recreation of the crime, but they'd never get confirmation from Katherine Knight, nor an explanation for her bizarre acts. Katherine claimed to have no recollection of what had happened. According to her, she'd arrived at the house to have sex with her lover. Everything after that was a blank.

Notwithstanding her apparent amnesia, Katherine Knight pled guilty at her trial in October 2001, at least sparing John Price's family the ordeal of hearing about his gruesome death. She was sentenced to life in prison without the possibility of parole, the first time that sanction had ever been imposed on an Australian woman. Knight is currently incarcerated at Mulawa Women's Correctional Centre.

For more True Crime books by Robert Keller please visit

http://bit.ly/kellerbooks

Printed in Dunstable, United Kingdom